The Divine Romance

Values and Ethics Series, Volume 4

The Divine Romance
Teresa of Ávila's Narrative Theology

Joseph F. Chorpenning, O.S.F.S.

Loyola University Press
Chicago

Loyola University Press
3441 North Ashland Avenue
Chicago, Illinois 60657

All Scripture quotations are from *The New American Bible* (Nashville: Thomas Nelson Publishers, 1971).

Cover: icon of St. Teresa in St. Teresa's Church in Chicago by Shirley Comptos. Photograph by Jill Salyards.

Library of Congress Cataloging-in-Publication Data

Chorpenning, Joseph F.
    The divine romance: Teresa of Ávila's narrative theology/
Joseph F. Chorpenning.
        p. cm. — (Values & ethics series; v.4)
    Includes bibliographical references and index.
    ISBN 0-8294-0732-4
    1. Teresa, of Ávila, Saint, 1515–1582. I. Title. II. Series:
Values & ethics series; v.4.
BX4700.T4C53 1992
248—dc20   92-2619
                                                                 CIP

To my teachers, most especially my first teachers in the Faith, my dear father and mother.

Table of Contents

Foreword

Teresa of Ávila, saint and first woman Doctor of the Church, was an enormously gifted woman. Among her myriad gifts was her talent for telling a story. Her stories continue to delight the imagination of an age grappling with a secularity that seeks a glimpse of the divine. Teresa had no doubt that God broke into her life often and intensely. Her vivid descriptions of her experiences of God helped her and her advisers to make some sense of the divine love that so energized her. Not until she was almost forty years old, however, did Teresa experience God in a way that adequately responded to her immense desire to live more fully under divine influence. God came to her at mid-life as the source and deepest center of her existence. She called this renewed life a "new book." With St. Paul she could say, "the life I live now is not my own; Christ is living in me" (Gal. 2.20). This new life enabled Teresa to share with others what God's love was accomplishing in her. These descriptions have fascinated God-seekers ever since divine love erupted in Teresa's heart. She found her life so centered on Jesus that, once she initiated her reform, she described herself as Teresa of Jesus.

When Teresa wrote her "autobiography," she revealed that she felt guilty about reading what we would call pulp romances. She and her mother hid these romantic tales of chivalry from a father who disapproved of them. My guess is that Teresa discovered in these stories of chivalry something of her own knack for turning out an exciting story. But there were other influences on Teresa the writer. When she wrote of her mid-life conversion, Teresa mentioned that she had read avidly the *Confessions* of St. Augustine, which had only recently been translated into Castilian. There is more than a little of Augustine in Teresa the storyteller. Moreover, the Scriptures were also a constant influence on Teresa's writing. The powerful story of Gethsemane had a place in her account of her conversion. The archetypal Mary Magdalene of the tradition also helped Teresa tell this story. Teresa was a romantic who kept her dreaming heart in tension with her feet-firmly-on-the-ground spirituality. But Teresa of Jesus never lost her flair as a great storyteller whether she was describing something quite human or telling with relish of the God who welled up so dramatically in her consciousness.

This gift for storytelling is the focus of Father Chorpenning's compelling theory that is presented so lucidly in his book. The author helps us to understand better Teresa's power to captivate the imagination of those who seek union with God. Teresa's writing is indeed a *divine romance* that allows the reader to find meaning in the faith experiences told so compellingly in her narratives. In the past theologians and literary scholars have collaborated all too little in their analyses of the mystical writings of the saint from Castile. That Joseph

Chorpenning's book is being published during the year of the Columbus quincentennial poses a challenge for further collaboration among the various disciplines that have found Teresa's narratives so gripping. Chorpenning's study of Teresa as the narrator of divine romance speaks to literary scholars as well as to theologians and shows how well his cross-disciplinary exploration of Teresa's work succeeds as a happy union of theological spirituality and literature. Father Chorpenning shows that it is time for disciplines to join hands in drawing out the meaning of this woman's experience. Her experience too often has been considered, from one or another horizon, to be too esoteric for the everyday reader. The latter will indeed gain from Chorpenning's book as well as from future collaborations among the disciplines. Father Chorpenning's study not only has a message for scholars but reads easily and swiftly for the nonscholar. His book will be a rewarding read for anyone interested in the wisdom of the woman who sang with gusto of the intersection of the divine with the human.

Like Teresa, Father Chorpenning tells a good story and, like her, he has a gift for effective symbols. One need read only a few pages into his book to discover Chorpenning's affection for Teresa. Yet he realizes that studies of Teresa's writings derive their chief worth from sending the reader back to Teresa's own texts. I came to Father Chorpenning's book reluctantly, since I prefer to go directly to the writings of the Spanish mystic. But I soon discarded my reluctance when I discovered that the author equips the prospective reader with a genuine taste for her writings. Teresa's stories are deceptively simple. One can miss much or can be easily misled without guidance. However, even the seasoned student of Teresa will find, under Chorpenning's direction, new horizons from which to more fully understand her mystical journey. Indeed, the novice reader will move more quickly into Teresa's narrative with the help of this able guide. Chorpenning enables one to discern with confidence the intent of Teresa's charming yet profound stories of God's lively and loving action in human life.

I liked and learned much from this study of Teresa's classical formulations of Carmelite mysticism. You will also. Father Chorpenning simply but surely directs one to a Teresa who cherished the story of Carmel, a story that the saint retells in a powerful new way. Originating about A.D. 1200 on Mt. Carmel, this story of the contemplative journey to God invites women and men of any and every tradition to listen to the wisdom of the Carmelite mystical tradition. Father Chorpenning's text will help you, as it has me, grasp better Teresa's vision of Carmelite mysticism's vital role in Christian discipleship.

Keith J. Egan
Saint Mary's College
Notre Dame, Indiana

Acknowledgments

I am grateful to Allentown College of St. Francis de Sales for a sabbatical grant during the 1988–89 academic year that made it possible for me to prepare this study. I also owe a debt of gratitude to Javier Herrero, Kenan Professor of Spanish at the University of Virginia; James J. McCabe, university librarian, Fordham University; and Elias L. Rivers, Leading Professor of Spanish and Comparative Literature at the State University of New York at Stony Brook, for carefully reading a draft of either a part or the whole of the book and for the helpful suggestions for improvement they offered. I thank my confrere Father Joseph G. Morrissey, O.S.F.S., and his secretary, Mary Alice Pusey, for their invaluable assistance in converting the electronic version of my manuscript into IBM compatible form.

An early version of chapter 1 was published with the title "Santa Teresa's *Libro de la vida* as Romance: Narrative Movements and Heroic Quest" in the *Revista Canadiense de Estudios Hispánicos* (14 [1989–90]: 51–64). I should like to thank the editor for permission to reproduce this material in revised and expanded form.

April 19, 1990
325th anniversary of the
Canonization of St. Francis de Sales

Introduction

The 1992 quincentennial of Columbus's discovery of America focuses attention on the Spanish Renaissance as an age of discovery and exploration of the New World. However, America was not the only new world discovered and explored by Spaniards during this period. The adventures of the conquistadores were paralleled by those of the Spanish mystics, who discovered and explored the interior and spiritual world of the soul and its relationship to God. Preeminent among these spiritual conquistadores is St. Teresa of Jesus or Teresa of Ávila as she is known in the English-speaking world. Mystic, reformer, and Doctor of the Church, Teresa wrote, in addition to various minor works and hundreds of letters, four major prose works on the spiritual life and her reform of the Carmelite Order: the *Book of Her Life* (begun in 1562 and completed in 1565), the *Way of Perfection* (c. 1566), the *Mansions of the Interior Castle* (1577), and the *Book of Her Foundations* (begun in 1573 and completed in 1582). As timeless as the message of Teresa's life and writings may seem to be, it unfolded in the context of the historical reality of sixteenth-century Spain.

Teresa in the Context of Her Times

Teresa de Ahumada was born in the medieval-walled, fortress-like city of Ávila of the Knights (*Ávila de los Caballeros,* so-called because of its long martial tradition), on March 28, 1515.[1] Her father was Alonso Sánchez de Cepeda, the son of Juan Sánchez, a wealthy cloth merchant and converted Jew (*converso*) from Toledo. In 1485, when Alonso was five years old, Teresa's grandfather and his family were "reconciled" by the Inquisition, established in 1478 by the Catholic Monarchs Ferdinand and Isabella to ensure the religious orthodoxy of *conversos* and thereby foster national unity. This reconciliation, which involved performing public penance, occurred because Juan "confessed that he had done and committed many serious crimes and delicts of heresy and apostasy against our holy Catholic faith."[2] What Juan's offenses were are unspecified in inquisitorial documents and hence are a matter of speculation. "He might have been guilty of donning a clean shirt on Fridays, the Jewish Sabbath, or been careful to strip away fat from his meat. Perhaps he refused to touch pork, but ate other meat in Lent, or was wont to hold the traditional valedictory supper before setting out on his frequent journeys. He may have recited one of the psalms without adding the Gloria obligatory for good Christians, or washed and shaved the corpses of deceased relatives according to Mosaic custom."[3] Eager to leave this humiliating experience behind, Teresa's grandfather eventually moved his family to Ávila to continue his cloth business. Teresa's father, Alonso

Sánchez, married in 1505, but two years later his wife, Catalina del Peso, died, leaving him two children. In 1509 Alonso, now twenty-nine, remarried; his wife was fifteen-year-old Beatriz de Ahumada. From this second marriage there were ten children, of which Teresa was the third.

The future saint was reared in a comfortable, middle-class world. Her parents were devout and virtuous Catholics. As a child, Teresa herself was dedicated to prayer, specifically the rosary, and good works such as almsgiving. Her close-knit family enjoyed reading, and so at an early age Teresa began to read the lives of the saints, particularly of women martyrs. At the age of seven, inspired by the stories of the martyrs, Teresa and her brother Rodrigo, who was closest to her in age, ran away from home in the hope of going to northern Africa, where they could be martyred by the Moors. However, an uncle found them on the road to Salamanca and brought them home. This episode from Teresa's childhood is immortalized in a splendid stained glass window in the chapel of the Convent of St. Teresa in Ávila that is built on the site of the saint's family home. Frustrated in their desire for martyrdom, Teresa and Rodrigo then tried to build a hermitage in the garden in back of their house so that they could pretend to be hermits; this garden is preserved at the aforementioned Convent of St. Teresa.

Like her contemporary St. Ignatius of Loyola, Teresa was extremely fond of reading the romances of chivalry, which were the bestsellers of the day.[4] In fact, one of Teresa's biographers, who was also her contemporary, the Jesuit Francisco de Ribera, reports that Teresa, in collaboration with her brother Rodrigo, actually wrote a romance of chivalry, now lost. According to Ribera, there was "much that could be said for it."[5] As we have seen in her earlier attempt to seek martyrdom, Teresa experienced literature with such intensity that it became life. Similarly, Teresa's reading of the knightly adventures and love stories of the chivalric romances led to a cooling of her childhood devotion, as she now began to cultivate her feminine charms and to plan a possible marriage. Teresa's mature judgment on this part of her life was that it was a time of vanity and frivolity.

The death of Teresa's mother in 1528 coincided with the future saint's entrance into adolescence. After her mother's death, Teresa came under the influence of a worldly female cousin about her own age; prior to her death, Teresa's mother had sought to keep Teresa from associating with this girl. Moreover, Teresa's inclination toward vanity and frivolity was encouraged by the servants in her home. Teresa's father became very concerned about the welfare of his daughter, and so he sent her to the Augustinian nuns' convent school of Our Lady of Grace, just outside Ávila.

Under the influence of the gentle, friendly nun charged with the supervision of the girls at Our Lady of Grace, Teresa began to consider a religious vocation. The turning point in Teresa's vocational discernment came while she was recovering from a fever at the home of her devout paternal uncle, Pedro de Cepeda, who dedicated himself to a life of prayer. Don Pedro introduced his young niece to devotional books. At first Teresa did not care for her uncle's books; her reaction was not unlike that of young Ignatius Loyola, who was less than enthusiastic when, while he was recuperating from his battle wounds, he asked for some chivalric romances to read and was given the only books available—a Spanish translation of Ludolph of Saxony's medieval *Life of Christ* and of Jacobo de Voragine's *Golden Legend*, a collection of the lives of the saints.[6] Similarly, just as Ignatius' spiritual reading was pivotal in his conversion and decision to become a soldier under the standard of Christ, Teresa's reading of the *Letters of St. Jerome*, several of which are exhortations to the eremitical life, moved her to make the decision she had been trying to avoid: to leave the world and enter a monastery as a nun. Teresa's father opposed her decision, but on November 2, 1535, at the age of twenty, Teresa fled her father's house and entered the Carmelite monastery of the Incarnation in Ávila. Don Alonso eventually accepted his daughter's decision. Teresa chose the Incarnation rather than the convent of Our Lady of Grace, which was the strictest and smallest in Ávila (it housed only fourteen professed nuns in 1532), because the latter's austerity and strict enclosure repelled her. Ironically, almost three decades later Teresa would leave the Incarnation to embrace a religious life—much like that led at Our Lady of Grace—in the first monastery of the reformed Carmel she would found in Ávila.

The Carmelite nuns at the Incarnation lived under a mitigated version of the primitive Carmelite rule that had required, among other things, strict poverty, solitude, and silence for the purpose of cultivating a life of prayer. At the large convent of the Incarnation (some two hundred persons, including servants and nuns' relatives, lived together at the Incarnation during Teresa's stay), days were set aside each week for fasting and abstinence, silence was prescribed to foster a spirit of continual prayer, and the Divine Office was celebrated with solemnity and splendor. However, no time was designated for mental prayer, distinctions of social class were maintained, and enclosure (cloister) was not strictly enforced. The nuns addressed one another by family names and, where appropriate, by the title "Doña." Nuns from the lower classes and those with limited economic means slept together in a common dormitory, while the wealthy lived in their own quarters, enjoying comfort and privacy. Because of her social position and the dowry her father gave her, "Teresa had a large private apartment at la Encarnación. . . . Situated on two levels and connected by a staircase, it included facilities for cooking and eating. Her youngest sister, Doña Juana, and several other relatives lived with her there."[7] Teresa often went out to act as a confidante or companion to actual or potential benefactors of the convent as well as to do fund-raising; because of her charming and attractive personality, Teresa frequently had visitors. Although quite happy as a nun, Teresa became critically ill within a year of entering Carmel. In 1538, Teresa appeared to be on the verge of death; an open grave awaited her, and only her father's refusal to part with the "corpse" saved her from being buried alive. Teresa eventually regained consciousness, but she remained an invalid and paralytic for three years and suffered from ill health for the rest of her life. Despite much speculation, modern scholars have been unable to identify the exact nature of Teresa's illness.

Once up and about, Teresa began to experience a protracted period of difficulty with prayer. During her illness, her uncle Pedro had given her the Franciscan friar Francisco de Osuna's *Third Spiritual Alphabet*, a guidebook for meditation. From this book Teresa learned about interior prayer; thus she was set on the path of prayer. But the life-style at the Incarnation undermined the solitude and recollection requisite for the life of prayer. Consequently, for more than a decade-and-a-half Teresa experienced considerable interior agitation. She felt that she was being torn apart by two inimical contraries: her friendship with God and her attachment to the world. In 1554, Teresa resolved this inner conflict when, moved by an *Ecce Homo,* an image of the wounded Christ in his passion, and the reading of St. Augustine's *Confessions,* she underwent a conversion. Severing all ties with worldly values and attitudes and resolved to follow the path to perfection, Teresa now started to practice prayer regularly and to avoid all that would distract her from it.

From this point on, Teresa led a new life. With St. Paul, she could say "the life I live now is not my own; Christ is living in me" (Gal. 2.20). Once Teresa began to walk steadfastly in the way of prayer, God granted her mystical forms of prayer and favors, for example, visions, raptures, and locutions. In one vision in 1556, Teresa saw the place in hell from which God's mercy had delivered her. This vision made a lasting impression on Teresa, who now sought to express her gratitude to God for his benevolence by founding a strictly enclosed (cloistered) monastery where the primitive Carmelite rule of poverty, prayer, and solitude would be observed and an apostolate of prayer for the Church, then besieged by the assaults of the Protestant reformers, would be carried out. The hallmark of Teresa's life would be an increasing spiritual generativity manifested by her activity as a monastic reformer/founder and a prolific spiritual writer. To understand and appreciate Teresa's contribution to the Church in these areas, it is necessary to situate her even more precisely in the religious landscape of sixteenth-century Spain.

On October 31, 1517, approximately two-and-a-half years after Teresa's birth, Martin Luther affixed his Ninety-five Theses to the door of the Castle Church at Wittenberg. However, in Spain there had been a Catholic reform movement that antedated Luther. In the late fifteenth and early sixteenth century, a program of religious reform and renewal was initiated by the Franciscan Cardinal Francisco Ximénez de Cisneros, who was Queen Isabella's confessor, archbishop of Toledo, primate of Spain, and Grand Inquisitor. A zealous patron of learning, Cisneros founded the University of Alcalá de Henares in 1508. Alcalá quickly became a renowned center of learning and humanism, where such well-known figures as Ignatius Loyola, St. John of Ávila, Lope de Vega, and Quevedo studied. Cisneros also financed the printing of the *Polyglot Bible* in six volumes (1514–17), which contained the first printed text of the Greek New Testament, and fostered the translation, publication, and diffusion of devotional literature in the vernacular. The recent invention of the printing press made available translations of the works of the Fathers of the Church, the Rhineland School, the *devotio moderna,* and the Italian mystics. The spiritual books that Teresa read and from which she benefited were the product of this movement to disseminate religious literature in Spanish.

With the death of Ferdinand in 1516 (Isabella had died in 1504), Charles I, soon to become emperor Charles V, inherited the thrones of the Catholic Monarchs, his maternal grandparents. Under Charles, the Catholic reform inaugurated by Cisneros continued. In the Spain of the 1520s, there was an openness to northern influences, particularly to the writings of the Dutch humanist Erasmus.[8] However, that openness came to an end when heterodox forms of spirituality surfaced; for example, the *alumbrados* (Illuminists) claimed direct illumination of the Holy Spirit and dispensed their adherents from the usual means of sanctification proposed by the Church. The Inquisition, originally established to ensure the orthodoxy of *conversos,* now broadened its scope to secure Spain from the Lutheran threat by extirpating any movement that, like Lutheranism, emphasized internal religion at the expense of outward ceremonial.[9] With the Council of Trent (1545–63), institutional reform was mandated for the universal Church, and the lines of demarcation were clearly drawn between Roman Catholicism and Protestantism. Trent's decrees were promulgated in Spain in 1564. Under Philip II, who succeeded his father Charles V in 1556, Spain became the paladin of the Catholic faith. Born at the end of the reign of the Catholic Monarchs, Teresa witnessed the changing religious climate of Spain during the reigns of Charles and Philip. But Teresa was not simply a passive spectator of these events—she was an active participant. Her reform of Carmel was aimed at aiding the Church in its self-reform and defense against Protestantism.

Learning was a key element in the Catholic reform. The primacy given to learning in the new orders founded in the sixteenth century and in the reform of the older orders, as well as of the theological formation of the secular clergy, was based on the conviction "that only a properly and appropriately educated minister was really competent to do the pastoral work for which Christians were everywhere crying out."[10] The Jesuits epitomize this aspect of the Catholic reform. Ignatius spent a decade studying at Barcelona, Alcalá, Salamanca, and Paris, because he discerned it was God's will that he spend "some time in studies in order to help souls."[11] Consistent with Ignatius' example, "the institution of the scholasticate and the provision for Jesuit universities, primarily for Jesuits themselves, made in the [Jesuit] constitutions have behind them a pastoral motive and are based on the conviction that the best work for souls could only be done by men thoroughly and appropriately trained not only in pure spirituality but also in the various sacred sciences."[12] In her own way Teresa shares this belief as well when she specifies, in the *Life*, chapter 13, that the ideal spiritual director is prudent, experienced, and learned. However, when, in the opening chapters of the *Way of Perfection*, Teresa explains the mission of the reformed Carmel, she confesses that she and her nuns are excluded from assisting the Church with learning, as theologians and preachers do, because they are women.

Teresa was probably the best educated of her nuns, and yet she had no formal education. Raised in an intensely oral culture but also influenced by a family tradition of reading and writing, Teresa, while still very young, learned to read Spanish with great fluency. But Teresa's own writing style does not imitate the spelling and syntax of the Spanish texts of devotional and imaginative literature she voraciously read; her style is the antithesis of the humanistic prose of spiritual writers of her day like the Dominican friar Luis de Granada or the Augustinian friar Luis de León, whose Spanish texts usually had a model, or subtext, in Latin.[13] Teresa's prose is "deliberately subliterate . . . an attempt to express Christian faith and humility by avoiding the normal written forms of basic Spanish words and by transcribing instead the pronunciations and phrases as heard from the mouths of illiterate peasants."[14] In this respect Teresa seems akin to St. Augustine, who invented in his *Confessions* and sermons a new colloquial eloquence to make the Scriptures available to all and to parallel the humility of the mystery of the Incarnation.[15] Teresa's written Spanish "is comparable, within an American context, to something composed by a writer of Black English, who deliberately tries to avoid the academic sound of white bourgeois correctness."[16] It is noteworthy that Luis de León, who, on the recommendation of St. John of the Cross, was commissioned to prepare the first edition of Teresa's works after her death and who had never met Teresa while she was alive, observed a curious similarity between the spoken Spanish of Teresa's nuns and her texts.[17]

At Our Lady of Grace, Teresa was taught cooking, sewing, and embroidery; undoubtedly, she was also given some religious instruction. As a novice at the Incarnation, Teresa was taught about the Carmelite Order, including its eremitical origins and its devotion to the Blessed Virgin and to the prophets Elijah and Elisha. She was also trained in the detailed, minute rubrics for the chanting of the Divine Office. Teresa never received formal theological training. Her doctrinal and literary formation is to be attributed to her vast reading—"somewhat unusual for a woman of her day"[18]— her relationship with her spiritual directors and confessors, and the preaching of the period.[19]

Compared with the learning of contemporary male theologians, Teresa's learning was meager. Teresa and her nuns could not assist the Church in its hour of need with learning. Rather, they would strive to be good friends of the Lord, who had so many enemies at this time, by living the evangelical counsels as perfectly as possible and by carrying out an apostolate of prayer for the Church. Teresa envisioned this mission of the reformed Carmel being realized in a strictly enclosed monastery of no more than thirteen nuns, where there would be no distinctions of social class and where the constitutive elements of the pristine Carmelite spirit—poverty, prayer, and solitude— would be maintained. This vision became a reality when, in the early hours of August 24, 1562, Teresa left the Incarnation to found the reformed Carmelite monastery of St. Joseph in Ávila. In contrast with the practice at the Incarnation, at St. Joseph's nuns abandoned their family names and titles; the only titles used were "Sister," or "Mother" in the case of the prioress. Hence, Doña Teresa de Ahumada became Teresa of Jesus. Initially, there was vehement opposition to St. Joseph's by the municipal officials of Ávila, who argued that this house, founded in absolute poverty, would place too great a strain on the city's already limited resources, and by ecclesiastical authorities, who viewed any emphasis on mental, as opposed to vocal, prayer with suspicion. But Teresa's reform and St. Joseph's prevailed. Teresa sought to revive and purify the contemplative dimension of Carmel. Thus her reform moved in a different direction from that of contemporary male orders, such as the Jesuits, Theatines, Barnabites, and Lazarists, who devoted themselves to specifically priestly pastoral ministry, especially preaching and administering the sacraments. It also differed from the activist female religious communities, such as the Visitandines, Ursulines, and Daughters of Charity, who, at least in their initial conception, sought to parallel their male counterparts.[20] Nonetheless, Teresa's reform was missionary: She set out to do battle with the heretics on her own terms "but in tandem with the theologians and the preachers and the soldiers of Philip II."[21] Each of Teresa's foundations, where the Blessed Sacrament was reserved in the chapel or adjacent church, was intended to replace those churches destroyed by the Protestants. In 1567, Teresa founded her second reformed monastery at Medina del Campo. Between that year and 1582, the year of her death, Teresa traveled all over Spain, enduring Castilian winters and Andalusian summers, to found fifteen more reformed monasteries. Because of the steady influx of vocations to her foundations as well as the need to ensure sufficient members to support the workload of these convents, Teresa was persuaded to increase the number of nuns in her communities from thirteen to fifteen and then to twenty-one. In her work as monastic founder and reformer, Teresa had to attend to a host of practical matters and details, from securing through diplomacy the necessary civil and ecclesiastical permission for her foundations to purchasing real estate to setting up housekeeping. Thus she integrated the contemplative and mystical life with ceaseless activity in the real, everyday world. Among the endearing characteristics of Teresa's personality are her natural intelligence, prudence, common sense, and refreshing ability to see the humorous side of life. Teresa's reform of the Carmelite nuns was paralleled by a reform of the friars. As is well known, Teresa's closest and most faithful collaborator in the latter endeavor was St. John of the Cross.

Teresa's postconversion spiritual generativity is manifested not only by her reform of Carmel and her foundations but also by her writings. In addition to 450 letters and a number of short pieces, Teresa wrote 4 major prose works, all of which are closely related to her reform and foundations: the *Life*, Teresa's autobiography; the *Way of Perfection*, the manifesto of the Teresian reform; the *Interior Castle*, Teresa's masterwork; and the *Foundations*, the chronicle of the dissemination of the Teresian Carmel.

Autobiography "is a shaping of the past. It imposes a pattern on a life, constructs out of it a coherent story. . . . Its significance is indeed more the revelation of the present situation than the uncovering of the past."[22] In the *Life* Teresa proposes to explain to her confessors and spiritual directors how she has become who she presently is—the recipient of mystical favors and a monastic reformer and founder—by recounting her life story from infancy to 1565. Like Augustine's *Confessions*, but unlike the autobiographies of the late medieval mystics Blessed Henry Suso and Margery Kempe, the *Life* is historical and concrete as Teresa deftly "entwines the story of her inward experience with that . . . of outward life, and her story leads naturally to the actual reform of conventual life and the founding of Saint Joseph's."[23] Moreover, Teresa's careful and delicate probing of the inner self, a characteristic shared with Augustine's *Confessions* as well as with contemporary writings such as the autobiographies of the Florentine artist Benvenuto Cellini and the Paduan physician Girolamo Cardano and the *Essays* of Michel de Montaigne, makes the *Life* modern.[24] The *Way of Perfection* is addressed to Teresa's nuns at St. Joseph's in Ávila, who requested her to instruct them in the practice of prayer. Not only does Teresa respond to this request, but she sets forth her ideal of Carmelite community life, teaching them in the process about temptations against which they must always be on guard. In the *Interior Castle* Teresa expounds, for the sisters at St. Joseph's and the ten other reformed monasteries she had founded up to 1577, a plan of individual spiritual development based on her own experience and her communal Carmelite ideal. Finally, in the *Foundations* the saint recounts her foundation of monasteries subsequent to St. Joseph's in Ávila, offers advice to prioresses on various matters, and gives biographical sketches of several early discalced Carmelite nuns and friars.

In the final chapter of the *Interior Castle*, Teresa states that the greatest favor God can grant a person is "a life that would be an imitation of the life His beloved Son lived."[25] It has been observed that "[the] last days of [Teresa's] life resemble the passion of Christ."[26] As Teresa's life drew to a close, she had to endure many hardships and much suffering, such as hostility from some of her prioresses, rivalry among the members of her own order, and a deterioration of the high standards she had set for her foundations. To the end Teresa worked tirelessly to realize her reform; she would die while on one of her many trips. On the evening of September 20, 1582, Teresa arrived in Alba de Tormes, a town northwest of Ávila, to oversee the election of a new prioress in the community, which was beset by problems. On September 29, Teresa suffered a severe hemorrhage; she never rose from her bed again. On the evening of October 4, the Mother of Carmel died. Modern physicians who have studied the surviving descriptions of Teresa's last illness believe the actual cause of death was cancer of the uterus. The following account of Teresa's death, based on the testimony of eyewitnesses given at her beatification and canonization proceedings, is found in the sixth lesson of the Second Nocturn in the old Roman Breviary:

> Fortified by the sacraments of the Church, exhorting her children in Christ to peace, love, and observance of the rule, she gave back her most pure soul to God, in the form of a dove. She died at the age of sixty-seven in the year 1582, on October 15, according to the corrected [Gregorian] form of the Roman calendar. Christ Jesus was seen present at her death bed amid hosts of angels. A withered tree outside her cell burst suddenly into bloom. Her body, surrounded by a fragrant liquid, has remained uncorrupted to this present day, and is still honored with pious veneration.[27]

Teresa's body is buried at Alba de Tormes. She was beatified by Pope Paul V on April 24, 1614, and canonized by

Pope Gregory XV on March 12, 1622, together with her fellow Spaniards Ignatius Loyola, Isidore of Madrid, Francis Xavier, and the Italian Philip Neri. On September 27, 1970, Pope Paul VI declared Teresa the first woman Doctor of the Church.

One of the requirements for being declared a Doctor of the Church is outstanding learning. In view of what has been said about Teresa's lack of formal education, it may seem strange that this title should be conferred upon her. Yet Teresa's writings present a depth and breadth of teaching on the spiritual life that is unique in the history of Christian theology. Neither Teresa's natural intelligence nor readings nor consultation with theologians suffice to explain from where she derives her elevated doctrine. For example, although Teresa had no formal training in Sacred Scripture and limited access to the Bible, her knowledge and use of Scripture is amazing. "Without any previous understanding of the meaning of a passage, without a knowledge even of the exact meaning of the words, the text being in Latin, she would suddenly penetrate, through mystical experience, to the deepest sense contained there and taste and enjoy it."[28] However, in the *Life*, chapter 26, we gain an insight into whence Teresa's learning came. In 1559, the Grand Inquisitor Fernando de Valdés issued the *Index of Prohibited Books,* which banned some of the books Teresa found beneficial. Teresa lamented this prohibition, but the Lord assured her. "'Don't be sad, for I shall give you a living book.' I was unable to understand why this was said to me, since I had not yet experienced any visions. Afterward, within only a few days, I understood very clearly, because . . . the Lord showed so much love for me by teaching me in many ways, that I had very little or almost no need for books."[29] Just as Ignatius Loyola was taught by God himself at Manresa,[30] Teresa was instructed by Christ himself. In the dedicatory letter to his edition of Teresa's works, Luis de León, the foremost biblical scholar of Golden-Age Spain, states that he considers Teresa's writings to be divinely inspired and to contain divine revelation. Moreover, Fray Luis points out, it is this woman, ignorant from an academic standpoint but learned in the divine mysteries, whom God raised up to combat the evils of the present age and to confound the learned of this world. "[It] seems, so far as I can judge, to have been God's will that [the devil and unbelievers] should be faced, not by a valiant man armed with learning, but by a poor woman who defied the devil and set up her standard against him and openly raised up people to conquer him and spurn him and trample him beneath their feet."[31] As Pope Paul VI declares in his apostolic letter proclaiming Teresa a Doctor of the Church, it is on account of her divine learning, transmitted to her by the Lord himself, that this title is conferred upon Teresa. "Notwithstanding her want of skill and knowledge to learn and teach, very frequently it was proven that, communing secretly with God, she was able to perceive, teach and commit to writing the most lofty realities. Christ alone was to her the foundation of wisdom and, as it were, the book of life."[32] Through her writings and example, Teresa continues to teach the Church the way to perfection.

Teresa, Reader and Author of Romances

"I never knew, or saw, Mother Teresa of Jesus while she lived on earth; but now that she lives in Heaven I do know her, and I see her almost continuously in two living images of herself which she left us—her daughters and her books."[33] This is the opening sentence of Luis de León's dedicatory letter to the first edition of Teresa's works (1588). Since Teresa's death over four hundred years ago, this is how many people have come to know her. Some have been privileged to make her acquaintance through her nuns, but many more have done so through her writings. It would be difficult to exaggerate the importance of Teresa's writings in making her known and in disseminating her spiritual doctrine. "Teresa's claim to sanctity, in fact, owed much to her writings, not merely the autobiographical works but those especially in which she expounded her methods of mystical prayer and devotion. She was believed to have composed her books under divine inspiration. Indeed, among the earliest and most numerous depictions of Teresa are those showing her as an author."[34] However, from the very beginning Teresa's texts have posed difficulties for her readers. Teresa's written Spanish was hard for her first editor, Luis de León, to read and understand. Teresa wrote rapidly under the pressure of time. In a letter she wrote to her younger brother, Lorenzo de Cepeda, in 1577, Teresa gives us a self-portrait. "You must not give yourself the trouble of re-reading the letters you write me. I never re-read mine. If a word here or there should have a letter missing, just put it in, and I will do the same for you, for your meaning is quite clear, and re-reading your letters would be a waste of time for you and all to no purpose."[35] Teresa's texts are further characterized by frequent ellipses, confused grammatical agreements, and long parenthetical statements that cause the reader to lose the train of thought. Teresa was well aware of her stylistic peculiarities; she expects her readers to be able to make necessary adjustments, read between the lines, and make sense of the text. When Luis de León confronted Teresa's writing, he found that it was the opposite of his own artistic humanistic prose. It was his recognition of the similarity of Teresa's written Spanish and her nuns' spoken Spanish that finally enabled him to understand and appreciate Teresa's literary style on its own terms.[36]

Four centuries later Teresa's texts continue to perplex her editors and translators. For example, Father Kieran Kavanaugh writes in the introduction to his and Otilio Rodríguez's recent translation of Teresa's works:

> Writing the way she talked, [Teresa] reflects the popular language of the Castilian people of her time. . . . As though her thoughts were jostling with each other for position, her sentences often become highly involved with parentheses and digressions, causing her sometimes to lose the thread—which never prevents her from leaping forward quickly and easily to a new thought. . . . Translating Teresa's sentences is often like working on puzzles, and some of the puzzles we can never be completely sure that we have solved. But by and large her meaning can be determined with certitude from the context.[37]

Similarly, modern Teresian scholars and commentators customarily fault the saint's writings for being diffuse and rambling and for lacking unity and coherence.[38] The general reader struggles with the same difficulties that the scholar encounters in trying to understand Teresa's texts and often registers the same complaints about them.

For many years it was a commonplace in Teresian scholarship that the saint was a spontaneous and ingenuous writer. But within the past fifteen years a new generation of scholars has subjected this stereotype to critical scrutiny by studying the rhetorical strategy of Teresa's prose works and has demonstrated that, far from being artless, Teresa is a masterful rhetorician and pragmatic stylist who carefully tunes her style to her audience.[39] Another characterization of Teresa the writer that is equally in need of reevaluation is that because she tends to be diffuse and rambling her works lack narrative structure and unity. A recent survey of the state of Teresian scholarship reveals that the narrative dimension of Teresa's works has been almost completely neglected by both literary scholars and theologians who investigate her writings.[40] This neglect is all the more surprising in view of the considerable interest in narrative in contemporary literary criticism and post–Vatican II theology. The primary objective of this book is to fill this lacuna in Teresian studies by offering a reading of Teresa's four major prose works as narratives that will challenge the traditional view that these works lack structure and unity. More specifically, I will approach the *Life*, the *Way of Perfection*, the *Interior Castle*, and the *Foundations* as romances.

As already noted, Teresa was an avid reader of stories or narratives. The narratives she read were of two (not unrelated) kinds: lives of the saints, which awoke in her the desire to undertake divine adventures, and the chivalric romances, which kindled in her a longing for worldly glory and the vanity of clothes, demeanor, and appearance. Teresa began to read the lives of the saints as a child, but she continued to find them a source of assistance and encouragement throughout her life, even at the most advanced stages of the spiritual life. Teresa's mother read the romances of chivalry secretly with her children, because her husband did not approve of them. In the *Life*, chapter 2, Teresa comments on this practice. "Perhaps she

[Teresa's mother] did this reading to escape thinking of the great trials she had to bear and to busy her children with something so that they would not turn to other things dangerous to them. . . . I began to get the habit of reading these books. . . . I didn't think it was wrong to waste many hours of the day and night in such a useless practice, even though hidden from my father. I was so completely taken up with this reading that I didn't think I could be happy if I didn't have a new book."[41] The chivalric romances so captivated Teresa that she even set out to write one herself. Actually these two kinds of stories are not that different—the lives of the saints Teresa read were adventure stories of divine chivalry. In fact, recent studies of hagiographic narratives have shown the close resemblance between their plot structure and that of medieval epic and romance.[42] In sixteenth-century Spain, the lives of the saints, with their emphasis on the miraculous, were clearly the religious counterpart of the chivalric romances and competed with them as bestsellers of the day.[43] Moreover, throughout the sixteenth century, especially in the latter half, there was a strong movement in Spain to rewrite and spiritualize the chivalric romances, for example, by making the knights a symbol of divine love.[44] In short, the narratives Teresa read, be they books of chivalry or lives of the saints, were romances.

In sixteenth-century Spain, romances were not simply read; they were lived. The world, images, and plots of romance dominated their readers' imaginations and lives. For example, in his *History of the Conquest of New Spain*, the chronicler Bernal Díaz del Castillo reports that when Cortés's soldiers first saw the spectacular Aztec capital of Tenochtitlán, site of present-day Mexico City, with its palaces, canals, bridges, and towers, they believed they were viewing a landscape from *Amadís de Gaula*, the most famous of the Spanish chivalric romances and the model for Cervantes' *Don Quixote*.[45]

Ignatius Loyola, who was steeped in the reading of the chivalric romances, took the models presented therein and tried to imitate their generous and exalted behavior even before his conversion; for example, he refused to participate in the sack of Nájera because this action was unworthy of a knight.[46] After his conversion, Ignatius continued to remain faithful to the models of the chivalric romances, which he spiritualized and fused with the example of divine knights such as Dominic and Francis of Assisi. Ignatius' vigil before the altar of Our Lady of Montserrat was inspired by two episodes from the chivalric romances—first, the penance of Amadís for the loss of his lady Oriana's love; and second, the vigil of Esplandián, Amadís's son, over his arms before a statue of the Blessed Virgin on the occasion of his consecration as a knight. "He [Ignatius] continued his way to Montserrat thinking, as he usually did, of the achievements he was going to perform for the love of God. As his thoughts were fully occupied with exploits, such as he read in *Amadís de Gaula* and other like books, similar thoughts also came to mind. He therefore determined to keep a night's vigil over his arms."[47] Subsequently, Ignatius is described as "Christ's new soldier."[48]

Finally, Teresa's imagination as well was pervaded by the world of romance. Years after reading the chivalric romances and allegedly writing one of these books as a teenager, Teresa had recourse to the images and landscape of these romances to present her doctrine. When Teresa explains her ideal of the reformed Carmel at the outset of the *Way of Perfection*, she images St. Joseph's monastery in Ávila as a castle or fortress, the walls of which are humility, surrounded by enemies, such as the world, opponents of reform, and heretics. Her nuns are Christ's knights, whose arms are poverty and simplicity and whose spiritual leaders are good captains.[49] However, before the monastery/castle can be used as a fortress against the common enemy, each nun within must conquer and fortify herself. Hence, the castle becomes the dominant icon of Teresa's masterwork, the *Interior Castle,* which has been described by Javier Herrero as "a lovely romance, . . . a love-story in which we find the echoes of innumerable books of chivalry":

> This castle is, in fact, our own soul, and, by nature, it has the beauty of the shining palaces that the medieval knights used to find in their adventurous journeys. It is inhabited by a powerful King. The outer reaches of the castle, however, have fallen in disrepair and are soiled by loathsome animals; but in its central court, the King has kept a lovely garden with an ever-flowing fountain and a delightful tree of life. . . . The end of the soul, her true happiness, will consist in conquering the castle (conquering herself) and directing her senses and faculties towards this central court that the King inhabits. . . . And this spiritual war, as in the more charming romances, ends in the happy union of the lovers. Once the soul has penetrated the most hidden recesses of the castle, and has there met her Lord and become one with Him, she finds herself the Lady of the most beautiful place, of the diamond-like abode which had been promised to her, in hope, at the beginning of her pilgrimage.[50]

These examples of the formative influence the chivalric romances exercised on their readers' imaginations and lives provide a strong rationale for approaching Teresa's works as romances.

Human experience has an intrinsically narrative, or story, quality about it. The story is the most common and universal means of communicating human experience, and human beings are essentially story listening/ reading and storytelling beings, with story listening/reading being a precondition for storytelling.[51] The stories Teresa read were chivalric and hagiographic romances and, hence, Teresa's telling of the story of her life, of her reform and foundations, of her Carmelite ideal, and of the development of the spiritual life can best be understood against the background of romance. The particular perspective from which I will view her works is the archetypal criticism of Northrop Frye, the most distinguished contemporary literary critic writing on romance. In the pages that follow, I will read Teresa's four major prose works with the assistance of Frye's grammar of narrative *The Secular Scripture: A Study of the Structure of Romance* (1976; Cambridge: Harvard University Press, 1982), supplemented by his *Anatomy of Criticism: Four Essays* (1957; Princeton, N.J.: Princeton University Press, 1971), *The Great Code: The Bible and Literature* (1981; New York: Harcourt Brace Jovanovich, 1982), and *Words with Power: Being a Second Study of the Bible and Literature* (New York: Harcourt Brace Jovanovich, 1990). The archetypes or formulaic units of romance identified and described by Frye stand out in Teresa's works, which, we will see, are sequences of romance archetypes. Consequently, the literary genre of romance provides us with a better appreciation than has been available to date of the narrative unity of Teresa's works.

I have written this book with various audiences in mind. One audience is the theologian, both spiritual and narrative. This study will show that Teresa's spiritual theology is essentially narrative in form; approaching Teresa's writings from the point of view of Frye's archetypal criticism also casts into relief the hallmarks of Teresa's reform and spirituality, for example, strict enclosure; the imitation of Christ; and the practice of the virtues of patience, detachment, humility, obedience, and love of neighbor. Narrative theology has sometimes been criticized for being imprecise and fuzzy because of its failure to determine the generic features of the narratives it discusses.[52] Frye's criticism provides the criteria to define precisely the genre of Teresa's narratives.[53]

A second audience I address is the literary scholar, who has often judged unfavorably the narrative structure and unity of these four works. My reading of Teresa's works seeks to provide a new way of defining their narrative unity by demonstrating that they are structured by the archetypes of romance.

A third audience that concerns me is the general reader. In this introduction I have tried to give the general reader a firm hold on Teresa and her historical context prior to the more specialized analysis of her works that follows. It is my hope that my commentary on Teresa's major works will be of use to the general reader as a companion piece that can be read alongside her original texts. For this purpose, I devote a chapter to each of Teresa's four major works, and I have made the format of these chapters uniform. After a brief overview of the state of the question of the coherence of Teresa's work and some introductory remarks, I divide the chapters of the work into groups that I correlate with Frye's archetypes. All quotations from Teresa's works are in English translation in order to make the commentary accessible to a wide audience. The commentary is rounded off with a conclusion in which, on the basis of the preceding chapters, I argue that images, archetypes, and narrative are essential and indispensable for recovering the richness and integrity of Teresa's spiritual theology. Finally, I provide a bibliographical guide to works on Teresa that have been published since 1982, the quatercentenary of her death.

A Note on Texts

All references to Northrop Frye's *The Secular Scripture, Anatomy of Criticism, The Great Code,* and *Words with Power* (full titles and bibliographical information are provided in the Introduction above), and to St. Teresa's works are given in the body of the text without further documentation. References to Teresa's works are to *The Collected Works of St. Teresa of Ávila, I: The Book of Her Life, Spiritual Testimonies, Soliloquies; II: The Way of Perfection, Meditations on the Song of Songs, The Interior Castle;* and *III: The Book of Her Foundations, Minor Works,* trans. Kieran Kavanaugh and Otilio Rodríguez (Washington, D.C.: Institute of Carmelite Studies Publications, 1976–85).

References to the *Life,* the *Way of Perfection,* and the *Foundations* are to chapter and section, e.g., 12.1 = chapter 12, section 1. As is well known, the *Way of Perfection* exists in two versions. The first version is conserved in the royal library of the Escorial; the second is kept in the Valladolid Carmel. All references in this book are to the Valladolid version. In the case of the *Interior Castle,* references are to mansions, chapter, and section, for example, 3.1.5 = 3rd mansions, chapter 1, section 5. References to prologues and epilogues are to section.

In preparing this study, I have constantly consulted the Spanish text of Teresa's works: Santa Teresa de Jesús, *Obras completas*, 7th ed. Efrén de la Madre de Dios and Otger Steggink, eds. (Madrid: Editorial Católica, 1982).

Chronology

Events in Spain and in Europe	Life of St. Teresa of Ávila
1469 October 19: Marriage of Ferdinand, King of Sicily and heir to the throne of Aragon, to Isabella, heiress of Castile	
1478 Establishment of the Spanish Inquisition	
1479 Ferdinand and Isabella, the Catholic Monarchs as Pope Alexander VI designates them in 1494, become joint rulers of Castile and Aragon	
	1485 Juan Sánchez, Teresa's paternal grandfather, a converted Jew (*converso*), and his family are reconciled by the Inquisition in Toledo

1486 Juan Sánchez moves his
      family to Ávila

1491 Birth of St. Ignatius
      Loyola
1492 Conquest of Granada, the
      last Moorish kingdom in
      Spain;
      Discovery of America;
      Publication of Antonio de
      Nebrija's *Grammar of the
      Spanish Language*, the first
      grammatical description
      of any modern European
      language, and of Diego
      de San Pedro's *Prison of
      Love*, the epitome of the
      Spanish sentimental
      romance;
      Birth of the Franciscan
      spiritual writer Francisco
      de Osuna
1499 Birth of St. Peter of
      Alcántara and of St. John
      of Ávila;
      Publication of Fernando
      de Rojas' novel-in-
      dialogue *Celestina*, the
      leading bestseller in the
      fiction category of the
      Spanish Golden Age
1504 Birth of the Dominican
      spiritual writer Luis de
      Granada;
      Death of Isabella

1505 Alonso Sánchez, Teresa's
      father, marries Catalina
      del Peso

1506 Birth of St. Francis Xavier;
Death of Columbus

    1507 Catalina dies, leaving
    Alonso with two chil-
    dren, María and Juan

1508 Cardinal Cisneros founds
the University of Alcalá
de Henares;
Publication of Rodríguez
de Montalvo's *Amadís de
Gaula*, the most famous
and popular of the
Spanish chivalric
romances;
Michelangelo begins
decoration of the Sistine
Chapel ceiling

1509 Henry VIII becomes King
of England

    1509 Alonso marries Beatriz de
    Ahumada, Teresa's
    mother

1510 Birth of St. Francis Borgia

1515 Birth of St. Philip Neri

    1515 March 28: Teresa is born
    in Ávila, the third of ten
    children from her father's
    second marriage (Teresa's
    siblings with year of
    birth: Hernando, 1510;
    Rodrigo, 1511; Lorenzo,
    1519; Antonio, 1520;
    Pedro, 1521; Jerónimo,
    1522; Agustín, 1527;
    Juana, 1528; and another
    child of whom nothing is
    known)
    April 4: Teresa is bap-
    tized in the parish church

of St. John the Baptist
in Ávila

1516   Death of Ferdinand and
        of Cardinal Cisneros;
        Charles of Ghent be-
        comes King of Spain
        (Charles I);
        Publication of St. Thomas
        More's *Utopia*
1517   October 31: Luther affixes
        his Ninety-five Theses to
        the door of the Castle
        Church at Wittenberg
1518   Cortés begins the con-
        quest of Mexico
1519   Charles I of Spain is
        elected Holy Roman
        Emperor and becomes
        Charles V
1521   While recuperating from
        a leg wound received
        while engaged in the
        defense of Pamplona,
        Ignatius Loyola begins
        reading a life of Christ
        and those of the saints,
        and undergoes conver-
        sion;
        Conquest of Mexico is
        completed
1522   March: Ignatius Loyola
        makes a general confes-
        sion and keeps vigil at
        our Lady's altar at the
        Benedictine abbey of
        Montserrat;

1522   Inspired by the stories of
        the martyrs, Teresa and
        her brother Rodrigo plan
        to run away from home
        in the hope of going to
        northern Africa, where

August-September: Ignatius begins writing the *Spiritual Exercises* at Manresa

1526 Publication in Spanish translation of *Manual of a Christian Knight* by the Dutch humanist Desiderius Erasmus, who enjoyed a popularity in Spain unprecedented in the rest of Europe

1527 Birth of Luis de León, the first editor of Teresa's writings; Publication of Francisco de Osuna's *Third Spiritual Alphabet*

1528 Publication of Baldesar Castiglione's *Book of the Courtier*

1530 Diet and Confession of Augsburg

1531 Pizarro begins the conquest of Peru

1533 Conquest of Peru completed

they can be martyred by the Moors

1528 Teresa's mother dies

1531 Teresa's father sends her to the Augustinian nuns' convent school of Our Lady of Grace

1532 Teresa leaves Our Lady of Grace because of illness

1533 While convalescing at her paternal uncle's house, Teresa reads the *Letters of St. Jerome* and discerns her vocation to religious life

1534 Ignatius Loyola and his companions make their vows at Montmartre in Paris; the Act of Supremacy declares Henry VIII head of the Church of England	1534 Teresa's brother Hernando leaves for Peru
1535 Execution of Thomas More	1535 Teresa's brother Rodrigo embarks for Río de la Plata; November 2: Teresa flees her father's house and enters the Carmelite monastery of the Incarnation in Ávila
1536 Death of Erasmus; Publication of Calvin's *Institutes of the Christian Religion*; Michelangelo begins the *Last Judgment*	1536 November 2: Teresa receives the religious habit at the Incarnation in Ávila
	1537 November 3: Teresa makes her religious profession of vows at the Incarnation in Ávila
1538 Birth of St. Charles Borromeo	1538 Teresa becomes critically ill and leaves the Incarnation to undergo treatment in Becedas; Teresa reads Francisco de Osuna's *Third Spiritual Alphabet*, given to her by her uncle, and begins to practice the prayer of recollection
	1539 Teresa returns to the Incarnation with a

1540   Papal approval of
Ignatius Loyola's consti-
tutions for the Society of
Jesus
1541   April 7: Francis Xavier
embarks from Lisbon for
India;
Calvin begins to organize
his church in Geneva,
and John Knox, his
reform in Scotland;
Unveiling of Michel–
angelo's *Last Judgment*;
Birth of El Greco
1542   May 6: Francis Xavier
arrives in Goa, India;
(June 24?): Birth of
St. John of the Cross

1544   January 29: Luis de León
makes his solemn profes-
sion of vows as an
Augustinian friar in
Salamanca
1545   Council of Trent opens
1546   February 18: Death of
Luther

1547   Birth of Cervantes

paralysis that will last for
three years
1540   Teresa's brothers Lorenzo
and Jerónimo leave on an
expedition to America

1542   Teresa recovers through
the intercession of
St. Joseph

1543   December: Death of
Teresa's father

1546   January 20: Teresa's
brother Antonio dies
from wounds suffered in
the battle of Iñaquito in
Peru;
Her brother Agustín
leaves for America

1548   Publication of Ignatius Loyola's *Spiritual Exercises*

1549   August 15: Francis Xavier arrives in Japan

1552   December 3: Death of Francis Xavier on the island of Sancian, off mainland China

1553   Jesuits found the College of San Gil in Ávila

1554   Publication of Luis de Granada's *Book of Prayer and Meditation*, the number one bestseller of the Spanish Golden Age (with twice as many editions as *Celestina*), and of the anonymous *Lazarillo de Tormes*, the first Spanish picaresque novel

1554   Moved by an *Ecce Homo*, an image of Christ during his Passion, and the reading of St. Augustine's *Confessions*, Teresa undergoes a profound conversion; Teresa begins to consult Jesuit confessors and directors

1555   Peace of Augsburg

1556   Charles V abdicates, and his son Philip II becomes King of Spain; July 31: Death of Ignatius Loyola

1556   Teresa is granted the favor of spiritual betrothal

1557   Teresa consults with Francis Borgia, who passes through Ávila; Teresa's brother Rodrigo is killed in battle in Chile

1559   In Spain the Grand Inquisitor Fernando de Valdés issues the *Index of Prohibited Books*;

1559   Teresa begins to experience the favor of intellectual visions of Christ

Publication of Jorge de Montemayor's *Diana*, the first Spanish pastoral romance

1560   Teresa begins to have imaginative visions of the risen Christ;
Teresa receives the favor of the transverberation (a vision in which she sees a cherub sent by God to pierce her heart with a fiery gold dart);
Peter of Alcántara visits Ávila and assures Teresa and others that her spiritual favors are divine in origin;
Teresa's famous vision of hell;
Discussion about a new foundation begins

1562   Wars of Religion between Huguenots and Catholics begin in France;
Construction of the Escorial, Philip II's palace-monastery, begins;
Birth of Lope de Vega;
October 19: Death of Peter of Alcántara

1562   Teresa writes the first draft of the *Book of Her Life*;
August 24: Foundation of the first reformed Carmelite monastery of St. Joseph in Ávila

1563   John of the Cross takes the Carmelite habit at St. Anne's priory in Medina del Campo;
December 4: Council of Trent closes;

1563   Teresa writes the *Constitutions* for St. Joseph's that eventually are approved by the bishop of Ávila and by the Pope (July 17, 1565)

St. Charles Borromeo
begins the reform of the
archdiocese of Milan

1564 Religious profession of
John of the Cross at St.
Anne's in Medina del
Campo;
Birth of Galileo and of
Shakespeare;
Death of Calvin and of
Michelangelo

1565 Teresa completes the
final version of the *Book
of Her Life*;
Teresa's brother Her-
nando dies in Colombia

1566 August: Revolt against
the Spanish crown begins
in the Netherlands with
Calvinist mobs running
wild and sacking
churches. The Duke of
Alba is dispatched with
an army to put down the
rebellion and to suppress
heresy

1566 Teresa finishes the first
and probably the second
redactions of the *Way of
Perfection*;
Teresa writes her *Meditations on the Song of Songs*;
Visit of the Franciscan
friar Alonso Maldonado,
who had been a mis-
sionary in Mexico, to
St. Joseph's in Ávila

1567 John of the Cross or-
dained a priest;
August 21: Birth of
St. Francis de Sales

1567 April 27: The Prior
General of the Carmelite
Order authorizes Teresa
to found other
monasteries;
August 15: Second
Teresian foundation—
St. Joseph's monastery
in Medina del Campo;

			Teresa meets John of the Cross in Medina del Campo and persuades him to join her reform
1568	The Church of the *Gesú* begun in Rome; Morisco revolt in Granada	1568	April 11: Third Teresian foundation—St. Joseph's monastery in Malagón; August 15: Fourth Teresian foundation— The Conception of Our Lady of Mt. Carmel monastery in Valladolid; November 28: First reformed foundation of the friars, Our Lady of Mt. Carmel priory at Duruelo, by John of the Cross; Teresa receives approval of her *Life* from John of Ávila
1569	Death of John of Ávila	1569	May 14: Fifth Teresian foundation—St. Joseph's monastery in Toledo; June 23: Sixth Teresian foundation—The Conception of Our Lady monastery in Pastrana; Teresa writes her *Soliloquies*
		1570	November 1: Seventh Teresian foundation—St. Joseph's monastery in Salamanca
1571	October 7: The Holy League's combined fleet, commanded by Philip II's	1571	January 25: Eighth Teresian foundation— Our Lady of the

half-brother, Don Juan de Austria, defeats the Turkish armada at Lepanto

1572 March 27: Luis de León arrested and imprisoned by the Inquisition for insisting on the primacy of the Hebrew text of the Old Testament and for translating the Song of Songs into the vernacular;
St. Bartholomew's Day massacre of the Huguenots;
September 30: Death of Francis Borgia

1573 The Duke of Alba is recalled from the Netherlands, and the Spanish crown changes its policy of repression to pacification and reconciliation

Annunciation monastery in Alba de Tormes;
October 14: Teresa becomes prioress at the Incarnation in Ávila

1572 November 18: Teresa receives the favor of spiritual marriage

1573 August 25: Teresa begins writing the *Book of Her Foundations*

1574 March 19: Ninth Teresian foundation—St. Joseph of Carmel monastery in Segovia;
April 6–7: Abandonment of Pastrana foundation (Pastrana nuns received at Segovia);
October 6: Teresa completes her term as prioress at the Incarnation

1575 Philip Neri founds the Congregation of the Oratory in Rome

1575 February 24: Tenth Teresian foundation— St. Joseph of the Savior monastery in Beas; May 29: Eleventh Teresian foundation— St. Joseph of Carmel monastery in Seville; Teresa's brother Lorenzo returns from America; December: Teresa is denounced to the Inquisition in Seville

1576 After almost five years of imprisonment, Luis de León is acquitted of all charges

1576 January 1: Twelfth Teresian foundation—St. Joseph's monastery at Caravaca; Teresa composes two depositions in her defense for the Inquisition in Seville; Fray Juan de la Miseria paints Teresa's portrait in Seville; August: Teresa writes *On Making the Visitation*

1577 El Greco arrives in Spain and settles in Toledo; December 3: John of the Cross is kidnapped by the Calced and imprisoned at Toledo

1577 June 2: Teresa begins to write the *Interior Castle*; November 29: Teresa finishes the *Interior Castle*

1578 John of the Cross composes most of the poem *The Spiritual Canticle*; August 4: King Sebastian of Portugal is killed at the battle of Alcázarquivir, leaving Philip II in direct line of succession to the Portuguese crown; August 17–18: John of the Cross escapes from his prison in Toledo

1579   Luis de León wins the tenured Chair of Biblical Studies at the University of Salamanca; El Greco completes *The Disrobing of Christ*

1580   Publication of Montaigne's *Essays*; Spain annexes Portugal, uniting the entire Iberian Peninsula under the rule of a single sovereign

1580   February 21: Thirteenth Teresian foundation—St. Anne's monastery in Villanueva de la Jara; June 26: Death of Teresa's brother Lorenzo; December 29: Fourteenth Teresian foundation—St. Joseph of Our Lady of the Street monastery in Palencia

1581   June 30: Fifteenth Teresian foundation— Blessed Trinity monastery in Soria

1582   Completion of the Escorial; John of the Cross begins to compose commentaries on his poems *The Spiritual Canticle, The Dark Night,* and *The Living*

1582   January 20: Sixteenth Teresian foundation— St. Joseph's monastery in Granada; April 19: Seventeenth Teresian foundation— St. Joseph of St. Anne

Flame of Love, all com-
pleted by 1587

1583   Publication of Luis de
León's *The Perfect Wife*
and *On the Names of
Christ,* Books 1 and 2

1584   Death of Charles
Borromeo;
John of the Cross com-
pletes the first redaction
of his commentary on
the poem *The Spiritual
Canticle* that he later

monastery in Burgos;
September 20: Teresa
arrives at Alba de Tormes
at six o'clock in the
evening;
September 29: Teresa goes
to bed critically ill and
announces that her death
is imminent;
October 3: Teresa receives
the Sacraments of Recon-
ciliation and of the Sick;
October 4: The Mother of
Carmel dies at nine
o'clock in the evening at
the age of sixty-seven
(The Gregorian calendar
is introduced in 1582,
and thus the day of
Teresa's death becomes
October 15, eventually
the date of her feast day.)

1583   Publication of the *Way of
Perfection*;
July 4: Nine months after
Teresa's death, her body
is exhumed at Alba de
Tormes and found to be
incorrupt

revises in a new redaction
(1585–86)

1585 Publication of Luis de
León's *On the Names of
Christ*, Book 3, and of
Cervantes' pastoral
romance *Galatea*

1585 October 17: Teresa's body
is again exhumed so it
can be transferred to
Ávila and is discovered to
remain incorrupt

1586 January 1: The Bishop of
Ávila opens the formal
investigation into the
heroicity of Teresa's
virtue;
September 1: the Royal
Council authorizes the
publication of Teresa's
writings

1588 Defeat of the Spanish
Armada;
Death of Luis de
Granada;
El Greco completes the
*Burial of the Count of
Orgaz*

1588 Publication of Luis de
León's edition, commis-
sioned by the Royal
Council, of Teresa's *Life,
Way of Perfection*, and
Interior Castle

1589 In a series of memorials
written to the Inquisi-
tion, the Dominican
inquisitor Alonso de la
Fuente alleges that
Teresa's writings are
heretical;
Luis de León composes a
defense of Teresa's
writings to refute the
charge of heresy

	1590 Publication of the Jesuit Francisco de Ribera's biography of Teresa
1591 August 23: Death of Luis de León; December 14: Death of John of the Cross	1591 At his death, Luis de León leaves an unfinished biography of Teresa that remains unpublished until 1883
1595 May 26: Death of Philip Neri	
1598 Birth of Bernini and of Zurbarán; Death of Philip II	
	1599 Publication of the Hieronymite Diego de Yepes' biography of Teresa
1609 July 27: Beatification of Ignatius Loyola; Publication of Francis de Sales' *Introduction to the Devout Life*	
1610 Canonization of Charles Borromeo	
1614 Death of El Greco	1614 April 24: Teresa is beatified by Pope Paul V
1619 October 25: Beatification of Francis Xavier	
1622 December 28: Death of Francis de Sales	1622 March 12: Teresa, together with Isidore of Madrid, Ignatius Loyola, Francis Xavier, and Philip Neri, is canonized by Pope Gregory XV

1675 Beatification of John of
      the Cross
1726 Canonization of John of
      the Cross
1926 John of the Cross is
      declared a Doctor of the
      Church

1970 September 27: Teresa is
      declared the first woman
      Doctor of the Church by
      Pope Paul VI

1

The *Life*

Teresian scholars have traditionally faulted the *Life* for its apparent lack of narrative unity. For example, E. Allison Peers considered the *Life* to be a compound of three elements: St. Teresa's exterior life, her interior life, and her objective spiritual teaching. For Peers, as well as later for Helmut Hatzfeld, Teresa's life story is interrupted by the "huge digression" of the allegory of the four ways of watering a garden that the saint employs in chapters 11–22 to explain the kinds of prayer she had experienced.[1]

In recent years commentators on the *Life* have tended to evaluate the question of its coherence more positively. Víctor García de la Concha has argued that the theme of God's grace and mercy serves to unify the *Life*, while Guido Mancini and Ricardo Senabre have proposed that the themes of prayer and humility, respectively, fulfill the same function.[2] However, the *Life* has an even greater coherence than has been perceived. When read in light of a recent grammar of narrative such as Northrop Frye's *The Secular Scripture: A Study of the Structure of Romance*, Teresa's autobiography reveals a clear narrative unity.

In *The Secular Scripture* Frye observes that Western culture has derived from the Bible a mythological universe consisting of four levels:

> The highest level is heaven, the place of the presence of God: this world is strictly beyond space, but may be symbolized, as in Dante's *Paradiso*, by the spatial metaphor of heaven in the sense of the sky, the world of sun, moon, and stars. The world above the moon is traditionally thought of as the world that escaped the fall, and is consequently what is left of the order of nature as God originally made it. Level two is the earthly paradise or Garden of Eden, where man lived before the fall. The associations of the word "fall" suggest that Eden is to be thought of as the highest point in the world, as it is geographically in Dante. Level three is the world of ordinary experience we now live in. Animals and plants seem to be well adjusted to this world, but man, though born in it, is not of it: his natural home is level two, where God intended him to live. Level four is the demonic world or hell, in Christianity not part of the order of nature but an autonomous growth, usually placed below ground (97–98; cf. *Words with Power*, 168–69).

The higher worlds (Eden and heaven) and the demonic world each have their own particular bodies of imagery. Among the images of the higher worlds and their demonic opposites (in parentheses) are: God (Satan), angels (demons), light (darkness), the paradise garden with the tree of life and the water of life (the wasteland and the sea of death), the bride and the bridegroom (the whore and the heathen), domesticated animals such as the sheep and the dove (wild animals, beasts of prey, reptiles), the city and the temple (the prison or dungeon and the furnace), and the straight road (the labyrinth or maze). The higher worlds are those of human desire, freedom, and fulfillment. The demonic world is one that desire totally rejects: It is a world of tyranny, nightmare, bondage, oppression, and confusion (*Anatomy of Criticism*, 141–50; *Great Code*, 139–68).

Frye contends that all stories in literature are complications of, or metaphorical derivations from, four narrative movements spread over this universe: first, the descent from a higher world, heaven or Eden; second, the descent to a subterranean or submarine world beneath this one; third, the ascent from a lower world to this one; and fourth, the ascent to a higher world, Eden or heaven (*Secular Scripture*, 97). The prime example of these movements is the Bible, particularly the life of the Messiah, which is the prototype of Christian romance. According to Frye, the Bible is a U-shaped story, beginning with descent and ending with ascent. However, within this great curve there is, in the Old Testament, a series of lesser ups and downs. In the New Testament this pattern is broken by a single act of redemption by a hero, the Messiah, who descends from heaven to be born on earth, goes through his ministry on earth, descends to the lower world to conquer death and hell after his death on the cross, ascends to the surface of the earth at his resurrection, and returns to heaven with his ascension (*Great Code*, 169–98; *Secular Scripture*, 163; *Words with Power*, 261–62).

In the *Life* Teresa describes her life both prior to and after her conversion experience of 1554 in terms of descents and ascents. In chapter 7 she speaks of her preconversion life as a series of fallings and risings that, if not for the mercy and grace of God, would have ended in hell. "[If] the Lord had not . . . given me the means by which I could ordinarily talk with persons who practiced prayer, I, falling and rising, would have ended by throwing myself straight into hell" (7.22; cf. 8.1–2). After her conversion, Teresa insists that God directly intervened in her life to break this pattern of ups and downs. "[Many] souls turn back since the poor things don't know how to help themselves. And I believe mine would have turned back, if the Lord hadn't so mercifully done everything; for your Reverence will see that there was no other ability in me than to fall and rise" (31.17). In fact, close examination of the *Life* reveals that it is a U-shaped story of metaphorical and/or visionary descents and ascents among the four levels of the universe defined by Frye: earth, hell, the earthly paradise of the soul or of St. Joseph's monastery in Ávila, and heaven.

Frye identifies a series of archetypes or formulaic units found in romance. Frequently romance begins in an idyllic world, "a world associated with happiness, security, and peace; the emphasis is often thrown on childhood or an 'innocent' or pre-genital period of youth" (*Secular Scripture*, 53; cf. *Words with Power*, 180). Next, a break in consciousness and loss of identity set the hero off on a descent to the demonic world that is often entered through some sort of opening such as a cave. Finally, the hero receives a "call," for example, a letter that restores the broken current of memory, prompts the hero to recover his or her identity, and enables him or her to recognize and be separated from the demonic. Thus, the hero is freed from the lower world in which he or she has been trapped or imprisoned and ascends to higher worlds (*Secular Scripture*, 97–157). These archetypes, as well as others identified by Frye and to which reference will be made below, such as the establishment of the ideal society and heroic combat with demonic forces, are outstanding in the *Life*. What follows is a correlation of the chapters of the *Life*, which I have divided into eight groups, and Frye's archetypes.

**Chapters 1–3:
An Idyllic World**

"It was a help to me to see that my parents favored nothing but virtue" (1.1).

Teresa begins her autobiography with an account of her family and childhood. As in romance, the world of Teresa's childhood is happy, secure, and peaceful—in short, idyllic. The environment in which Teresa was reared was ideal. Her parents, she tells us, were devout and virtuous, and her brothers and sisters, with the exception, Teresa says, of herself, resembled their parents in this regard. But Teresa's self-deprecation is not supported by the information she gives about her childhood. She was fond of reading lives of the saints, which inspired in her a desire for martyrdom. She was accustomed to giving alms and praying the rosary. However, one fault that Teresa mentions is that, like her otherwise virtuous mother, she was addicted to reading the romances of chivalry, a practice inveighed against by numerous sixteenth-century moralists.[3] Ironically, the genre of romance provides a better understanding of the narrative unity of Teresa's autobiography than we have had to date.

At the outset of the *Life*, Teresa's identity is defined: She is the friend of God, the one whom God calls and cares for by giving her devout parents, awakening in her the desire for martyrdom, putting good books in her hands, and watching over her to guard her against the devil. The object of her quest is also made known. As a child, Teresa wanted to run off to the land of the Moors to be martyred so that she would be able "to enjoy very quickly the wonderful things I read there were in heaven" (1.4). Teresa's life will be a quest to attain heaven. Furthermore, her identity and quest are intimately related, because the friend of God "is chosen for God's own house and kingdom" (10.3).

When Teresa is thirteen, her mother dies. Now the happiness, security, and peace of her childhood home are threatened by the absence of a mother to guide Teresa through the troubled years of adolescence, by Teresa's friendship with a frivolous female cousin, and by the presence of unscrupulous servants. It could be expected that this "openness" of her home life would be the entrance through which Teresa would embark on a descent into hell. But this descent is averted by Teresa's father sending her to the Augustinian nuns' convent school in Ávila, where she recovers "the good habits of early childhood" (2.8).

By the time Teresa finished her schooling, she was wrestling with a religious vocation, because she considered the monastery to be "the best and safest state" (3.5) for her. Teresa's reasoning again highlights the object of her quest: "that the trials and hardships of being a nun could not be greater than those of purgatory and that I had really merited hell; that it would not be so great a thing while alive to live as though in purgatory; and that afterward I would go directly to heaven, for that was my desire" (3.6).

Chapters 4–8:	"[It] seems that . . . it is
Loss of Identity and	**a step on the way**
Descent into Hell	**toward hell"** (7.3).

Teresa's first nine months in the Carmelite monastery of the Incarnation, however, surpassed her expectations. Although the change in life-style did injury to her health, Teresa was content and at peace: She read spiritual books, sought out solitude, confessed frequently, and meditated regularly on the Passion of Christ. Moreover, Teresa was even led to some initial experience in mystical prayer. But eventually Teresa loses her first fervor. For the next eighteen years, she repeatedly frustrated God's work in her life, even to the point of abandoning mental prayer. "I began to fear the practice of prayer. It seemed to me that, since in being wicked I was among the worst, it was better to go the way of the many, to recite what I was obliged to vocally and not to practice mental prayer and so much intimacy with God" (7.1). During this extended period, a "battle and conflict between friendship with God and friendship with the world" (8.3) raged within Teresa.

By failing to practice mental prayer regularly, Teresa's identity as the friend of God became diffused. Just as in romance a break in consciousness and loss of identity precipitate the hero's descent into the demonic world (*Secular Scripture*, 129, 145; *Words with Power*, 233, 266), so too the diffusion of Teresa's identity leads her on a descent into hell. Teresa acknowledges that because she

abandoned mental prayer, "I merited to be with the devils" (7.1), and "I was heading just about straight to perdition" (7.11). Further, Teresa's life during this time was a
veritable hell. "I should say that it is one of the most
painful lives, I think, that one can imagine; for neither
did I enjoy God nor did I find happiness in the world.
When I was experiencing the enjoyments of the world, I
felt sorrow when I recalled what I owed to God. When I
was with God, my attachments to the world disturbed
me. This is a war so troublesome that I don't know how I
was able to suffer it even a month, much less for so many
years" (8.2). Teresa's perception that this segment of her
life was a descent into hell, and that she deserved to be
with demons and in hell, was confirmed by her famous
vision of hell in 1556, reported in chapter 32 of the *Life*.
"[While] I was in prayer one day, I suddenly found that,
without knowing how, I had seemingly been put in hell.
I understand that the Lord wanted me to see the place
the devils had prepared there for me and which I
merited because of my sins. . . . The Lord desired me to see
with my own eyes the place His mercy had freed me
from" (32.1, 3).

The hero of romance often enters the demonic world
through an opening (*Secular Scripture,* 119). Teresa makes
it clear that she also descends into hell through an opening, the unenclosed, that is, the open monastery of the
Incarnation.[4] Teresa expected that the monastery would
be a metaphorical purgatory on the way to heaven; however, for her, it became "a step on the way toward hell"
(7.3). What accounts for this transformation? In order to
answer this question, it is necessary to review briefly the
origins of monasticism in general and of the Carmelite
Order in particular.[5]

The *Life of St. Antony*, written shortly after Antony's death in A.D. 356 by St. Athanasius, the great bishop of Alexandria who was Antony's apprentice in the ascetic life, is the oldest monastic biography we possess. However, it is more than a biography; it is a kind of rule and model in narrative form for monks that became the inspiration of monasticism. First, Antony's life makes clear that monasticism consists of withdrawal from the world to a remote place (the desert in Antony's case) and from those things that attach the would-be monk to the world (marriage and family, property and material possessions, concern for esteem in the eyes of humanity, social position, and temporal power). Second, monastic life emphasized the practice of continual prayer, solitude, poverty, asceticism, manual labor, and humility. By its very nature, monasticism pertained to higher worlds. As we will see in greater detail later in this chapter, the monastic life was considered to be a return to Eden. Athanasius records that the monasteries that sprang up in the desert, due to the inspiration of Antony, were "populated with monks who left their own people and registered themselves for citizenship in Heaven."[6] But the monastic life is not realized without painful and powerful opposition from demonic forces that strive to destroy the earthly paradise of the monastery, just as they did Eden. For example, the devil seeks to break the resolution of the monk "by putting him in mind of his property, . . . the attachments of kindred, the love of money, the love of fame, the myriad pleasures of eating, and all the other amenities of life,"[7] that is, all those things of the world from which the monk has freed himself for the service of God. Thus, the world and the things of the world are the weapons the devil uses in his effort to conquer the monk and the monastery so that he can make them part of the demonic world.

When the Carmelite Order was founded circa 1200 in Palestine, the hallmarks of its life and rule were principally those common to the monastic tradition: the following of Christ that, for these inhabitants of the Holy Land, had the special connotation of a literal tracing of Christ's footsteps on earth and of a faithful vigil in his native land; obedience to a prior; solitude—each Carmelite was to have a separate cell where, unless attending to some other duty, he was to meditate day and night on the law of the Lord and watch in prayer; individual recitation of the psalter; daily celebration of the Eucharist; poverty and manual labor; silence; and fasting and perpetual abstinence from meat. After Saracen invasions forced the early Carmelites to migrate to Western Europe, their rule was twice relaxed, resulting in the modification of the contemplative tradition of the Order. In Teresa's view, based on her own experience, the invasion of the Incarnation by the world—the devil's principal weapon in the war he waged against the religious life since the beginning of monasticism—accounts for its transformation from a metaphorical purgatory on the way toward heaven to "a step on the way toward hell" (7.3). This invasion occurred precisely because "the rule was not kept in its prime rigor" (32.9) at the Incarnation. For example, strict poverty was not observed, for "the monastery had a lot of comfort since it was a large and pleasant one" (32.9). Teresa herself had a large private apartment, complete with a parlor and cooking facilities. Distinctions of social class and lineage were maintained at the Incarnation. Teresa and other nuns of her social class not only enjoyed privileges denied nuns of humbler origins but were also greatly concerned about prestige and honor, "things that

are usually esteemed in the world" (7.2). The Incarnation
was literally "open" because the nuns (Teresa being among
them) "often went out" (32.9), and there were many
visitors who came to exchange gossip in the salon like
atmosphere of its parlor.[8] Not only did this openness
undermine the solitude and recollection demanded by
the life of prayer, it allowed evil influences to enter the
monastery. "It is a pity that many who desire to withdraw
from the world, thinking they are going to serve the Lord
and flee worldly dangers, find themselves in ten worlds
joined together without knowing how to protect themselves or remedy the situation. For youthfulness, sensual-
ity, and the devil incite them and make them prone to
follow after things that are of the very world" (7.4). Teresa
confesses that because of the openness permitted at the
Incarnation, for many years she sustained an extremely
dangerous relationship with an unnamed person who
was the source of the greatest distraction to her. The
character of this friendship was made manifest on one
occasion when a large toad, an animal belonging to the
fauna of the demonic world, moved toward Teresa and
this person (7.7–8).[9] Although Christ himself sternly re-
buked Teresa for maintaining the friendship, she continued to do so and hence exclaims when she reflects back
on this episode "to what extent I merited hell for such
outrageous ingratitude" (7.9).

The openness of the Incarnation then explains its
metamorphosis from purgatory to "a step on the way
toward hell" (7.3). In this unenclosed monastery Teresa's
identity as the friend of God is diffused by her abandoning prayer and by her being affected by the evil influences
to which she was exposed therein; thus, her life becomes
a descent into hell. "[It] seems to me it did me great harm
not to be in an enclosed monastery. For the freedom that

those who were good were able to enjoy in good con-
science (for they were not obligated to more since they
did not make the vow of enclosure) would have certainly
brought me, who am so wretched, to hell, if the Lord with
so many remedies and means and with His very special
favors had not drawn me out of this danger" (7.3).

Chapters 9–10: Recovery of Identity and Ascent to Higher Worlds

"I remained for a long time totally dissolved in tears" (9.8).

In romance the hero frequently receives a "call" that
prompts the individual to recover his or her identity,
escape from the lower world in which he or she is trapped
or imprisoned, and ascend to higher worlds (*Secular Scripture*, 136–37, 156–57). Teresa receives two such calls in
1554. First, she is profoundly moved by an *Ecce Homo:*

> It happened to me that one day entering the
> oratory I saw a statue they had borrowed for a
> certain feast to be celebrated in the house. It
> represented the much wounded Christ and was
> very devotional so that beholding it I was utterly
> distressed in seeing Him that way, for it well
> represented what He suffered for us. I felt so
> keenly aware of how poorly I thanked Him for
> those wounds that, it seems to me, my heart
> broke. Beseeching Him to strengthen me once
> and for all that I might not offend Him, I threw
> myself down before Him with the greatest out-
> pouring of tears (9.1).[10]

Second, reading the *Confessions*, she is struck by St. Augustine's struggle:

> As I began to read the *Confessions*, it seemed to me I saw myself in them. I began to commend myself very much to this glorious saint. When I came to the passage where he speaks about his conversion and read how he heard that voice in the garden, it only seemed to me, according to what I felt in my heart, that it was I the Lord called. I remained for a long time totally dissolved in tears and feeling within myself utter distress and weariness. Oh, how a soul suffers, God help me, by losing the freedom it should have in being itself; and what torments it undergoes! I marvel now at how I could have lived in such great affliction. May God be praised who gave me the life to rise up from a death so deadly (9.8).

Struggling, as she was, with the conflict between her friendship with God and her attachment to the world, Teresa experienced herself as a divided self, an experience that, it has been noted, facilitated her identification with Augustine, who immediately prior to his conversion spoke of the existence and conflict of two wills within him.[11] It was painful for Teresa to read about Augustine's struggle, because it resonated in her own life. Both of these "calls" leave Teresa dissolved in tears and act as catalysts for the recovery of her identity as the friend of God, for her liberation from the spiritual impasse—the metaphorical and psychological hell—in which she was trapped for almost two decades, and for her ascent to the higher worlds of the earthly paradise and heaven.

These two calls effect a conversion in Teresa. As a result, she begins to practice mental prayer regularly, which enables her to recover her identity as the friend of God and to avoid occasions of sin; hence, she recognizes and separates herself from the demonic. "[After] these two instances of such great compunction and weariness of heart over my sins, I began to give myself more to prayer and to become less involved with things that did me harm, although I still did not avoid them completely; but—as I say—God was helping me turn aside from them" (9.9). Teresa describes her life from this point on in these terms. "This is another, new book from here on—I mean another, new life. The life dealt with up to this point was mine; the one I lived from the point where I began to explain these things about prayer [in chapter 10] is the one God lived in me—according to the way it appears to me—because I think it would have been impossible in so short a time to get rid of so many bad habits and deeds" (23.1). Indicative of the value Teresa ascribes to her "new life" is the number of chapters she apportions to it in the *Life*—three times as many as she devotes to her life up to 1554! The imbalance in chronological years is striking: chapters 1–9 encompass thirty-nine years, from 1515 to 1554, while chapters 10–40 cover only eleven, from 1554 to 1565.

In his discussion of the themes of ascent, Frye comments that "With the restoration of memory, and the continuity of action that goes with it, we have reached, so to speak, the surface of the earth, and are well on the way toward the higher themes of ascent, which take us toward the recovery of original identity" (*Secular Scripture*, 147). Teresa's conversion brings her to the surface of the earth as well as initiates her ascent to higher worlds. In chapter 10 Teresa states that the "joys of prayer must be like those of heaven" (10.3). Once Teresa starts to meditate regularly and to avoid the occasions of sin, God intervenes dramatically to guide the course of her life. If earth, purgatory, and hell dominate chapters 1–8 of the *Life,* the earthly paradise and heaven prevail in chapters 10–40. Now the curve of Teresa's life commences an ascending movement that affirms and solidifies her original identity as the friend of God.

| Chapters 11–22: Ascent to the Earthly Paradise of the Soul | "[This Lord of ours] will often come to take delight in this garden" (11.6). |

When Teresa begins to follow resolutely the "path of prayer" (11.1; cf. 13.1, 22), God almost immediately grants her supernatural forms of prayer and favors, transporting her to the higher worlds of the earthly paradise and heaven and expressing her friendship with him. "Since His Majesty was not waiting for anything other than some preparedness in me, the spiritual graces went on increasing in the manner I shall tell" (9.9). In chapters 11–22 Teresa explains the development of the soul's relationship to God in prayer by means of the allegory of the four ways of watering a garden. The garden (soul) and its plants (the virtues) flourish to the degree that they are cared for and cultivated:

> The beginner must realize that in order to give delight to the Lord he is starting to cultivate a garden on very barren soil, full of abominable

weeds. His Majesty pulls up the weeds and plants good seed. Now let us keep in mind that all of this is already done by the time a soul is determined to practice prayer and has begun to make use of it. And with the help of God we must strive like good gardeners to get these plants to grow and take pains to water them so that they don't wither but come to bud and flower and give forth a most pleasant fragrance to provide refreshment for this Lord of ours. Then He will often come to take delight in this garden and find His joy among these virtues (11.6).

For the garden (soul) and its plants to grow, they must be watered. Teresa specifies that the garden can be watered in four ways, which correspond to the "four degrees of prayer" (11.8) the Lord granted her: buckets of water drawn from a well (meditation); a bucket-type, water-wheel turned by hand (the prayer of quiet); diverting a stream along irrigation ditches (the prayer of the sleep of the faculties); and rain from heaven (the prayer of union).

Through prayer, Teresa's soul becomes the earthly paradise. Recently it has been suggested that elements of Teresa's representation of the landscape of the garden (soul) may be derivative of the chivalric romances she read, for example, the description of the garden of the castle of Miraflores in *Amadís de Gaula*.[12] The watering allegory of chapters 11–22 is also a virtual rewriting of the story of the garden of Eden in Genesis 2–3.[13] There are several obvious parallels between these two texts: [1] God plants the garden of Eden and of the soul (Gen. 2.8; *Life*, 11.6), [2] God makes the trees and plants of these gardens grow (Gen. 2.9; *Life*, 11.9; 14.5), [3] there are four waters associated with each garden (Gen. 2.10–14; *Life*, 11.7), [4] God appoints humankind as the gardener who is to care for and cultivate these gardens (Gen. 2.15; *Life*, 11.6–7), and [5] God is present in both gardens to enjoy them (Gen. 3.8; *Life*, 11.6). Essentially, it is God's presence that makes both gardens a paradise; in the paradisal state, humanity is on familiar and intimate terms with God. At this point, however, the two garden stories diverge. In Genesis, humanity shows itself to be undeserving of God's presence by disobeying and consequently is expelled from Eden. By contrast, in the *Life* the earthly paradise of Teresa's soul is preserved and maintained by prayer and avoiding the occasions of sin. Frye points out that "The closer romance comes to a world of original identity, the more clearly something of the symbolism of the garden of Eden reappears" (*Secular Scripture*, 149). The paradisal imagery of chapters 11–22 of the *Life* manifests iconically Teresa's recovery of her fundamental identity as one who is on familiar and intimate terms with God.

Chapters 23–29: Ascent Heavenward

"'No longer do I want you to converse with men but with angels'" (24.5).

Prayer and avoiding the occasions of sin lead not only to the restoration of the earthly paradise of Teresa's soul but also to her becoming the recipient of various mystical favors that are the focus of chapters 23–29 of the *Life*. Teresa explains at the beginning of chapter 23, "Now, then, when I began to avoid occasions and devote myself to prayer, the Lord . . . started to grant me favors" (23.2). These favors are associated with the higher paradise of heaven.

After her conversion, Teresa becomes convinced that she is on the road to heaven rather than the road to hell. "I saw that I was a completely different person. I could not desire another path, but I placed myself in the hands of God that He would carry out His will completely in me; He knew what suited me. I saw that on this road I was being led to heaven, that previously I had been going to hell" (27.1). This conviction is confirmed by the divine favors she receives. For example, the first time God grants Teresa the favor of rapture, she hears these words, " 'No longer do I want you to converse with men but with angels' " (24.5). Thus, the Lord freed her from earthly attachments from which she could not free herself. Moreover, God gives Teresa the "heavenly gift" (27.9) of infused knowledge—how, in heaven, he and the soul communicate without speaking:

> [There] is also another way in which God teaches the soul and speaks to it. . . . It is a language that belongs so to heaven that here on earth it is poorly understood, no matter how much we may desire to tell about it, if the Lord does not teach us through experience. The Lord puts what He wants the soul to know very deeply within it, and there He makes this known without any image or explicit words. . . . it seems to me that the Lord in every way wants this soul to have some knowledge of what goes on in heaven. I think that just as in heaven you understand without speaking . . . so it is in this vision. For God and the soul understand each other only

through the desire His Majesty has that it understand Him, without the use of any other means
devised to manifest the love these two friends
have for each other (27.6–10).

Teresa also has imaginative visions of the risen and
glorified Christ, that is, as he presently is in heaven (e.g.,
28.1–4; 29.4; 38.17–18). The saint describes and comments on one of these "heavenly visions" (29.4) as follows: "One feastday of St. Paul, while I was at Mass, this
most sacred humanity in its risen form was represented to
me completely, as it is in paintings, with such wonderful
beauty and majesty. . . . I only say that if there were
nothing else to provide delight for one's vision in heaven
than the exalted beauty of glorified bodies, this vision
would be very great glory, especially the vision of the
humanity of Jesus Christ, our Lord" (28.3). Finally, Teresa,
who previously by her own admission "merited to be with
the devils" (7.1), has a vision of a cherub sent by God to
pierce her heart with a fiery gold dart for the purpose of
leaving her "all on fire with great love of God" (29.13).
This supernatural increase in love of God and the subsequent impulses of divine love make Teresa long for death
so that she can be inseparably joined to God in heaven.

**Chapters 30–31:
The Heroic Defense of
the "New Life"**

**"Why shouldn't I have
the fortitude to engage
in combat with all of
hell?" (25.19).**

At this point in the *Life*, Teresa could not seem to be
further removed from the demonic world. Yet in chapters
30 and 31, she comes into closer and more direct contact

with Satan and his minions than she does prior to her conversion. When the first monk and "Father of Monasticism," St. Antony, withdrew from the world to lead a life of intense prayer and asceticism, he encountered violent opposition from demonic forces.[14] Similarly, Teresa's "new life" (23.1) is strongly contested by the demonic world that afflicts her with apparitions of the devil and various demons, severe interior and exterior pain, and acute anxiety that is, in Teresa's opinion, "a kind of copy of hell" (30.12). Teresa's attitude, when confronted by the powers of darkness after her conversion, contrasts sharply with the "servile fear" (3.6) of hell that motivated her to become a nun. Confident of God's omnipotence in her life, Teresa is calm and unafraid in the face of demonic forces. "If this Lord is powerful, as I see that He is and I know that He is, and if the devils are His slaves . . . what evil can they do to me since I am a servant of this Lord and King? Why shouldn't I have the fortitude to engage in combat with all of hell?" (25.19).[15]

The mission of the hero of romance is to restore paradise on earth by undertaking a series of adventures and combats with demonic forces. The success of the hero derives from a current of energy that is partly from him or her and partly outside him or her (*Secular Scripture,* 67, 139, 150, 172). Teresa's defense of her "new life" against the fierce interior and exterior assaults of the demonic world casts into relief the heroic character of her quest to attain heaven. She is victorious in this combat because of the presence of God in her; her victory establishes again her identity as the friend of God. It is God, neither Teresa nor the devil, who guides the movement of her life.

Chapters 32–36: Ascent to the Earthly Paradise of St. Joseph's Monastery

"[This] house was a paradise of delight for [God]" (35.12).

As already noted, Teresa's vision of the place she deserved in hell, recorded in chapter 32 of the *Life*, confirmed her perception that prior to her conversion she was on the road to hell. God's purpose, Teresa tells us, in granting her this vision was that she see the place from which his mercy had delivered her. This experience had a strong impact on Teresa, who now sought to respond to God's benevolence on her behalf. "I was thinking about what I could do for God, and I thought that the first thing was to follow the call to religious life, which His Majesty had given me, by keeping my rule as perfectly as I could" (32.9). Thus was born Teresa's dream of founding an enclosed monastery, in which the primitive Carmelite rule of poverty, prayer, and solitude would be observed, and an apostolate of prayer for the Church— then besieged by the attacks of the Protestant reformers— would be carried out. "From this experience also flow the great impulses to help souls and the extraordinary pain that is caused me by the many that are condemned (especially the Lutherans, for they were through baptism members of the Church)" (32.6). This dream became a reality with the foundation of St. Joseph's monastery in Ávila on August 24, 1562.[16] Teresa founded St. Joseph's in the face of tremendous civil and ecclesiastical opposition that she repeatedly attributes to the instigation of the devil,[17] who has been relentless in the war he has waged against the religious life since the origin of monasticism.

Consequently, the foundation of St. Joseph's is another testimony to Teresa's heroism. Like the hero of romance who confronts and overcomes various obstacles to restore paradise on earth, Teresa resisted and surmounted the opposition she encountered to recreate the earthly paradise in the enclosed monastery of St. Joseph's.

To grasp the significance of St. Joseph's as the earthly paradise, it is necessary to know that it was a commonplace in the monastic literature of the Patristic period and the Middle Ages that the monastic life was a return to, a reentry into, the earthly paradise. This theme typically would be developed as follows. Like Eden, the monastery is a *hortus conclusus* (enclosed garden), separated from the world and closed again on God.[18] The angels populated Eden, and the monk is called to live with and to be like the angels, particularly by chastity, which reinstates him to the earthly paradise. The cloister is a paradise of delights, where the monk is nourished on the bread of angels, the Eucharist and the fruit of the tree of life, the Scriptures.[19] The earthly paradise of the monastery is both a reflection and anticipation of the true paradise of heaven.[20]

In continuity with this well-established tradition, Teresa describes St. Joseph's in these terms in chapter 35 of the *Life*: "O greatness of God! Often I am amazed when I consider how particularly His Majesty wanted to help me found this little dwelling corner for God. I believe this is what it is; it is an abode in which His Majesty delights, for He once said to me while I was in prayer that this house was a paradise of delight for Him" (35.12). Hence, St. Joseph's, like the garden (soul) of chapters 11–22 cultivated by prayer, reestablishes the earthly paradise.[21] St. Joseph's is like Eden in that it is enclosed, separated from the world, and closed again on God. The sole desire and aim of its inhabitants is "to rejoice solely in Christ, one's Spouse" and "to be alone with Him alone" (36.29). The earthly paradise of St. Joseph's is also both a reflection and an anticipation of the true paradise of heaven, as Teresa indicates in the *Way of Perfection*: "This house is a heaven, if one can be had on this earth" (13.7).

Frye remarks that "[romance] has its own conception of an ideal society, but that society is in a higher world than that of ordinary experience" (*Secular Scripture*, 150). In the *Life* a similar notion of the ideal society emerges. For Teresa, the ideal is the enclosed monastery of St. Joseph's in Ávila, which is the antitype of the unenclosed monastery of the Incarnation. The latter is "a step on the way toward hell" (7.3), while the former is paradise on earth and "the road of perfection" (35.14) that leads to heaven. St. Joseph's was the prototype for Teresa's subsequent monastic foundations (see *Foundations*, 3.18; 9.1). By the foundation of St. Joseph's, then, Teresa severs the connection that existed between the monastery and the world at the Incarnation and restores the monastery to the higher worlds to which it properly belongs.

In romance the hero's evolution of consciousness benefits humanity: The restoration of the earthly paradise signifies the recovery of order and harmony for humanity (*Secular Scripture*, 172–73). Likewise, St. Joseph's is the fruit, the universalization and incarnation, of Teresa's complex spiritual development charted up to this point in the *Life*. At St. Joseph's, Teresa and her nuns live on familiar and intimate terms with God, as humankind did in Eden and as God intended humankind to live (*Secular Scripture*, 98). Thus in the earthly paradise of St. Joseph's, humanity is restored to friendship and intimacy with

God, and the Church is aided in its efforts at reform and its defense against Protestantism.

Chapters 37–40:	"It seemed to me I was
The Completion of	brought to heaven"
the Heroic Quest	(38.1).

It has been commented that in chapters 37–40 of the *Life* "the reader is left with the notion that the Castilian Saint was living more among the Church triumphant of heaven than the Church of this earth."[22] In this final section of her autobiography, Teresa attains the object of her heroic quest: heaven. Indeed, she reports not only that the Lord had shown her "how great the difference is in heaven between the joy of some and the joy of others" (37.2), but that on one occasion she had a rapture in which she was actually transported to heaven:

> One night, being so ill that I wanted to excuse myself from mental prayer, I took my rosary in order to occupy myself in vocal prayer. I tried not to recollect my intellect, even though externally I was recollected in the oratory. When the Lord desires, these devices are of little avail. I was doing this for only a short while when a spiritual rapture came upon me so forcefully that I had no power to resist it. It seemed to me I was brought into heaven, and the persons I saw there were my father and mother. I saw things so marvelous—in as short a time as it takes to recite a Hail Mary—that I indeed remained outside myself; the experience seemed to me too great a favor. I say it lasted a short time, but perhaps it took a

little longer; the impression is that the time was very short (38.1).

Subsequently, Teresa testifies, the Lord revealed "greater secrets" (38.2) to her. In various raptures she saw the Divinity enthroned in heaven (39.22), was given infused knowledge "how there is only one God and three Persons" (39.25), and was shown the Assumption of the Virgin Mary into heaven and "the happiness and solemnity with which she was received, and the place where she is" (39.26). Once while at prayer, Teresa senses that she is "surrounded by angels and very close to God" (40.12). Teresa has also extraordinary intercessory power comparable to that of the saints in heaven: Her prayer restores sight to the blind, heals the sick, and draws souls from sin (39.1–5). In one of the concluding paragraphs of the *Life*, Teresa declares her present perspective on life from the "little dwelling corner" and "paradise" (35.12) of St. Joseph's: "Since I am among a few holy companions and am not in the world, I observe as though from up high. . . . And [the Lord] has given me a kind of sleep in life, or it almost always seems to me that I am dreaming what I see" (40.22).

To sum up, the *Life* is a U-shaped story that concludes at a higher level than where it starts. The archetypes of romance are outstanding in the *Life*: the idyllic world of youth, the loss of identity and descent into hell through an opening, the "call" to recover identity and to ascend to higher worlds, the ascent to the earthly paradise and to heaven, the establishment of the perfect society, and the heroic combat with demonic forces. Teresa employs these archetypes, which she would have encountered in her reading of chivalric and hagiographic romances,[23] to recount the story of her own spiritual adventures aimed at the reform of the Carmelite Order and the Church. The *Life* not only has the shape of a romance but itself takes on an archetypal character. Approached from the perspective of romance, the *Life* exhibits a remarkable narrative unity.

2

The *Way of Perfection*

There is a fair amount of agreement among Teresian scholars regarding the structure and content of the *Way of Perfection*.[1] After a preamble that consists of the preface and chapters 1–3, which set forth the purpose of the Teresian Carmel, the *Way* is divided into three parts: chapters 4–15, a discussion of love of neighbor, detachment, and humility that St. Teresa avers are the foundations of prayer; chapters 16–26, an exposition of specific kinds of prayer, such as mental and vocal prayer, and contemplation; and chapters 27–42, a commentary on the prayer of prayers, the Our Father. In short, according to this consensus, the *Way* is a didactic treatise on prayer composed by Teresa for the instruction of her nuns. However, traditional scholarship has given little attention to the work's imagery, save the most well-known images of the castle, the palace, and the chess game, and no consideration to its possible narrative unity. When read from the perspective provided by Northrop Frye's theories on romance, the *Way* reveals a narrative unity as well as a rich imagery that is integral to this unity.

Over four decades ago, E. Allison Peers remarked that although all of Teresa's major works are "inseparably linked" to the *Life*, the *Way* "arises even more directly out of the *Life* than any of the others," for it was composed because the nuns at St. Joseph's in Ávila did not have access to the *Life*.[2] More recently, Kieran Kavanaugh has noted that at the end of the *Way* Teresa "implies that she has thought of this book as an introduction to her *Life* by asserting that those who have reached the fount of living water will find her *Life* very beneficial and receive much light from it."[3] From the perspective of narrative, the *Way* also "directly arises" out of the *Life*; however, it is neither a substitute for nor introduction to but a continuation of the *Life*, because Teresa's presentation in the *Way* of her ideal of Carmelite conventual life, epitomized by the earthly paradise of St. Joseph's monastery in Ávila, significantly replicates her own spiritual development, as it is recorded in the *Life*. Consequently, a number of the same archetypes found in the *Life* recur in the *Way:* the demonic world's contesting of the recovery of identity, the heroic defense of identity against the demonic world, separation from the demonic world, and the ascent to the higher world of heaven. These archetypes structure the *Way* and give it narrative unity.

In this chapter we will see that the *Way* develops the archetypal world that was introduced in the *Life*. The struggle between the eternal and unchanging, higher and demonic worlds is situated more firmly in the historical context of the sixteenth century. Teresa builds a castle or fortress around the earthly paradise of St. Joseph's to defend it against invasion by the demonic world. From this stronghold Teresa and her nuns devote themselves to an apostolate of prayer in order to assist the Church in its defense against Protestantism. Thus, they become participants in the cosmic battle between the higher and demonic worlds: God, his friends (Teresa and her nuns), and soldiers (preachers and theologians), must defend the Church and monastery against the attacks of Satan and his henchmen (the reformers, their followers, and those who would invade St. Joseph's such as vain and indiscreet confessors).

| Chapters 1–3: A Contest with the Demonic World | "The wiles of the devil are many for women who live a very cloistered life" (Prologue 3). |

In chapters 30–31 of the *Life*, Teresa had to defend heroically the recovery of her original identity as the friend of God and her postconversion "new life" (*Life*, 23.1), against fierce interior and exterior attacks by the demonic world. Similarly, at the outset of the *Way*, it is clear that Teresa and her nuns, under her leadership, are intensely engaged in defending the ideal society and restoring the earthly paradise of St. Joseph's that is being vigorously contested and assaulted by the demonic world. The prologue of the *Way* reveals that Teresa is concerned with teaching her nuns not only "some things about prayer" (1) but also "some remedies for certain common, small temptations of the devil" (2) because "[the] wiles of the devil are many for women who live a very cloistered life" (3). In fact, heroic combat with the demonic world becomes the leitmotif of the *Way*, as Teresa's constant references throughout the text to waging war and fighting battles against the devil attest.[4]

Teresa founded St. Joseph's, she tells us in chapter 32 of the *Life*, for the purpose of expressing her gratitude to God for his mercy in delivering her from the place in hell that she thought she deserved. More specifically, this gratitude was to be expressed by the observance of the primitive Carmelite rule of poverty, prayer, and solitude and an apostolate of prayer for a Church besieged by the attacks of the Protestant reformers. In chapters 1–3 of the *Way*, Teresa returns to this point even more emphatically.

In the initial chapter of the *Way*, Teresa is keenly distraught over the Church's present troubles. "At that time news reached me of the harm being done in France and of the havoc the Lutherans had caused and how much this miserable sect was growing. The news distressed me greatly, and, as though I could do something or were something, I cried to the Lord and begged Him that I might remedy so much evil" (1.2).[5] But what could Teresa do about the "harm" being done to the Church? Violence was futile. The efforts of preachers and theologians to defend the Church with learning excluded her. Teresa comes to realize that the best way for her to help the Church in its hour of need was by living out her fundamental identity as the friend of God, an identity to which the Lord himself had called her. Likewise, the nuns of Teresa's reformed Carmel would share her identity. Their vocation was to be good friends of the Lord. Teresa puts it this way: "All my longing was and still is that since [the Lord] has so many enemies and so few friends that these few friends be good ones" (1.2). The primary way Teresa and her sisters would express their friendship with the Lord would be by following the evangelical counsels as perfectly as possible. Hence, Teresa resolves "to do the little that was in my power; that is, to follow the evangelical counsels as perfectly as I could and strive that these few persons who live here [at St. Joseph's] do the same" (1.2). Moreover, Teresa and her community would carry out an apostolate of prayer for those entrusted with the defense of the Church: preachers and theologians. "Since we would all be occupied in prayer for those who are the defenders of the Church and for preachers and for learned men who protect her from attack, we could help as much as possible this Lord of mine who is so roughly treated by those for whom He has done so much good; it seems these traitors would want Him to be crucified again and that He have no place to lay His head" (1.2).

We have seen that in the *Life* Teresa's identity as the friend of God, postconversion "new life," and restoration of the earthly paradise of St. Joseph's were challenged by the devil. In the *Way* it is evident that Teresa conceives of history as a cosmic battle between, on the one hand, God and his Church and, on the other, Satan and the powers of darkness. The conflicts with the demonic world that Teresa experienced in her personal and spiritual development and in her work as monastic reformer and founder are part of this cosmic battle. For Teresa, the Protestant reformers and their followers are friends and disciples not of the Lord but of Satan (see 1.4); thus, their attacks upon the Church are those of the devil himself. As the Lutheran theologian Jürgen Moltmann has observed, Teresa placed the "'Protestant danger' . . . in the realm of apocalyptic horrors."[6] Teresa and her small community of nuns participate in this apocalyptic confrontation by striving to be good friends of the Lord, by being faithful to their vows, and by praying for the Church and its defenders. In chapter 35 of the *Life*, St. Joseph's is the earthly paradise because there—as a result of the observance of the primitive Carmelite rule of poverty, prayer, and solitude—Teresa and her nuns live on familiar and intimate terms with God, as humankind did in Eden and as God intended humankind to live. However, in chapter 3 of the *Way*, the earthly paradise of St. Joseph's becomes a castle and a fortified city in order to manifest iconically that not only is it part of the defense of the Church, but that the ideal society of St. Joseph's itself must be defended against the demonic world:[7]

> It has seemed to me that what is necessary is a different approach, the approach of a lord when in time of war his land is overrun with enemies and he finds himself restricted on all sides. He withdraws to a city that he has well fortified and from there sometimes strikes his foe. Those who are in the city, being chosen people, are such that they can do more by themselves than many cowardly soldiers can. And often victory is won in this way. At least, even though victory is not won, these chosen people are not conquered. . . .

> But why have I said this? So that you understand, my Sisters, that what we must ask God is that in this little castle [i.e., St. Joseph's] where there are already good Christians not one of us will go over to the enemy and that God will make the captains of this castle or city, who are the preachers and theologians, very advanced in the way of the Lord (3.1–2).

If Teresa and her nuns are to carry out their promised apostolate of prayer for the Church, St. Joseph's must remain secure as an enclosed monastery of the primitive Carmelite observance. Therefore, Teresa and her nuns must engage in combat with the demonic world to preserve St. Joseph's. Teresa admonishes her nuns that, both as a community and as individuals, they must be "interiorly fortified" (3.4). To this end, Teresa turns her attention in chapters 4–15 of the *Way* to three ways in which the devil could enter St. Joseph's and make it a hell: particular friendships, attachments, and a concern for honor.

Chapters 4–15: The Defense of St. Joseph's

"It is necessary to watch and pray always" (7.6).

Prayer was the prerequisite for Teresa to maintain her identity as the friend of God. As we have seen in chapters 4–8 of the *Life*, when Teresa failed to practice mental prayer regularly, her identity became diffused, and she began a descent into hell. When, after her conversion experience of 1554, Teresa resumed the practice of mental prayer, she recovered her identity and embarked on ascents to the higher worlds of the earthly paradise and heaven. It is not surprising then that in chapter 4 of the *Way* Teresa singles out prayer as the primary means whereby her sisters will maintain the identity they share with her as friends of God. "Our primitive rule states that we must pray without ceasing. If we do this with all the care possible—for unceasing prayer is the most important aspect of the rule—the fasts, the disciplines, and the silence the order commands will not be wanting" (4.2).[8] From her years at the monastery of the Incarnation, Teresa knew how easily the devil could enter a monastery, introduce evil influences that destroy the environment necessary for prayer, and make the monastery "a step on the way toward hell" (*Life*, 7.3). Teresa is determined that this not occur at St. Joseph's, and for this purpose she instructs her sisters in chapters 4–15 about three "things that are necessary for those who seek to follow the way of prayer" (4.3). "The first of these is love for one another; the second is detachment from all created things; the third is true humility, which, even though I speak of it last, is the main practice and embraces all the others" (4.4). The vices that are the opposites of these virtues are the means by which the devil may enter St. Joseph's.

The first snare of the devil against which the community of friends of the Lord at St. Joseph's must be on guard is particular friendships.[9] At St. Joseph's, Teresa says, "all must be friends, all must be loved, all must be held dear, all must be helped" (4.7). Teresa's disapproval of particular friendships in contemplative communities is based on her own experience at the Incarnation of how such excessive love "little by little . . . takes away the strength of will to be totally occupied in loving God" (4.5). Teresa is concerned about two kinds of such friendships: first, friendships between one member of the community and another community member; and, second, the relationship between a nun and her confessor. With regard to the former, Teresa states:

> I believe this excessive love must be found among women even more than among men; and the harm it does in the community is well known. It gives rise to the following: failing to love equally all the others; feeling sorry about any affront to the friend; desiring possessions so as to give her gifts; looking for time to speak with her, and often so as to tell her that you hold her dear and other trifling things rather than about your love for God. For these great friendships are seldom

directed toward helping one love God more. On
the contrary, I think the devil gets them started
so as to promote factions in religious orders. For
when love is in the service of His Majesty, the
will does not proceed with passion but proceeds
by seeking help to conquer other passions (4.6).

The greatest harm this kind of particular friendship causes
to a community is that it detracts from the solitude and
silence required for prayer (see 4.9). Consequently, the
identity of the individual nun and of the community as a
whole is threatened. For Teresa, such friendships are a
form of domination (4.7) and slavery (4.8), images associated with descent into the demonic world (*Anatomy of
Criticism*, 147–50; *Secular Scripture*, 104, 134). Positively,
Teresa exhorts her sisters to strive to acquire spiritual love
for one another, "a love with no self-interest at all. All
that it desires or wants is to see the other soul rich with
heavenly blessings" (7.1). This love is an imitation of
"that love which the good lover Jesus had for us" (7.4). It
is the opposite of "when we desire love from some person" because in that case "there is always a kind of seeking our own benefit or satisfaction" (6.5).

Another relationship that requires circumspection is
that of a nun with her confessor:

I want to speak now about the love that is spiritual, that which is not affected by any passion;
where passion is present the good order is thrown
into complete disorder. And if we deal with
virtuous persons discreetly and moderately, especially confessors, we will benefit. But if you
should become aware that the confessor is turning toward some vanity, be suspicious about

everything and in no way carry on conversations with him even though they may seem to be good, but make your confession briefly and bring it to a conclusion. And it would be best to tell the prioress that your soul doesn't get on well with him and change confessors. That would be the most proper thing to do—if you can do it without hurting his reputation (4.13).

Such a confessor is an affliction for the entire community:

[The] harm the devil can here cause is great, and only very slowly is it recognized; thus perfection can be gradually vitiated without one's knowing why. For if this confessor wants to allow room for vanity, because he himself is vain, he makes little of it even in others. May God, because of who He is, deliver us from such things. A situation like this would be enough to disturb all the nuns because their consciences tell them the opposite of what their confessor does. And if they are restricted to only one confessor, they don't know what to do or how to be at peace. For the one who should be calming them and providing a remedy is the one who is causing the harm. There must be a lot of these kinds of affliction in some places. It makes me feel great pity, and so you shouldn't be surprised if I have tried to explain this danger to you (4.16).

Teresa repeatedly emphasizes that an indiscreet and vain confessor is the means the devil uses to cause great harm to a community (see 4.14–16; 5.1, 5), even to the point of

turning it into "a hell" (4.15). She insists that "this entrance" be "taken away from the devil" (5.5).

The second trap of the devil that Teresa wants her
sisters to avoid is attachments to relatives (other than
parents), to self and comfort, and to honor. Again, Teresa
was aware from her experience at the Incarnation that
these attachments are obstacles to the cultivation of an
atmosphere conducive to prayer and recollection (see
8.3). Giving themselves totally to the Lord was to be the
only concern of the nuns at St. Joseph's. "And since in
[the Lord] are all blessings . . . let us praise Him very
much, Sisters, for having brought us together here where
the only concern is to give ourselves entirely to Him"
(8.1). As a result, Teresa challenges her nuns to a process
of detachment that involves an unceasing "war against
ourselves" (12.1), since the devil constantly tempts them
to be self-indulgent (10.5), to suppose that penances harm
them (10.6), and to imagine pains (11.2).

Closely related to the virtue of detachment is that of
humility, the remedy for concern for honor, namely, the
third way in which the devil seeks to enter St. Joseph's
(see 12.6–9).[10] Teresa regards concern for honor and privileges of rank such as were observed at the Incarnation to
be "a pestilence from which great evils arise" in monasteries (12.4; cf. 13.3). Honor and privileges of rank are contrary to the humility modeled for our imitation by Christ
(10.4; 12.6) and turn a monastery into a hell (27.6; 36.3–
5). For Teresa, true humility manifests itself in several
concrete ways: by accepting an obedience to do a lowly
task without complaint (12.7), by reflecting on the pun-
ishment our sins deserve and on God's mercy (12.6), and
by not excusing oneself when blamed without fault (13.1;
15.1–2). The humility Teresa urges her nuns to practice is

an imitation of Christ's own for, she says, "to enjoy a part in His kingdom and want no part in His dishonors and trials is nonsense" (13.2).

If Teresa's nuns follow the counsel she gives them regarding love of neighbor, detachment, and humility, St. Joseph's will not only be the earthly paradise but also a heaven on earth. "This house is a heaven, if one can be had on this earth. Here we have a very happy life if one is pleased only with pleasing God and pays no attention to her own satisfaction" (13.7). Otherwise, the monastery will become "a hell here on earth" that will precede eternal perdition in the next life (13.5). Finally, to ensure the devil does not enter the monastery by means of "little things" (12.8) like excessive love, attachments, and concern for honor, Teresa enjoins her nuns: "it is necessary to watch and pray always, for there is no better remedy than prayer for discovering these secret things of the devil and bringing them to light" (7.6).

Chapters 16–26: Separation from the Demonic World	"[By] means of so good a path the Lord will draw him to the haven of light" (19.1).

In romance the demonic world is "a dark and labyrinthine world" (*Secular Scripture,* 119), and ascent from this world occurs when there is "separation between the lower world and those who are destined to escape from it" (*Secular Scripture,* 137). Teresa would have her sisters separate themselves from the dark and labyrinthine demonic world by following the "path of prayer" (20.3) that God illuminates (21.9) and that leads to the "haven of light" (19.1). Although the image of the road/ way/path is ubiquitous in Teresa's writings,[11] nowhere is it more so than in chapters 16–26 of the *Way*. In these chapters it functions as an image of ascent that is the antitype of the "demonic labyrinth of lost direction" (*Great Code,* 161; cf. *Anatomy of Criticism,* 150). While this road may be divided into "different paths" (20.1)—vocal prayer, mental prayer, and contemplation—and sometimes be "rough and uneven" (18.2), the soul that travels upon it is on a "divine journey which is the royal road to heaven" (21.1).

Prayer is to be the "main occupation" (17.1) and "business" (20.4) of Teresa's sisters; the Carmelite rule commanded the nuns "to pray unceasingly" (21.10). As Teresa knew well from her own experience, prayer is the means whereby the identity of the friend of God is maintained. Prayer then preserves the nuns from a loss of identity that would set them on a descent to the demonic world (see 20.4), separates them from this lower world, and places them on a sure and safe path to the higher world of heaven. But Teresa has no illusions about the arduousness of the path of prayer. It is the "path of tribulation" (18.1) along which God leads those whom he greatly loves: his friends. Consequently, this journey requires courage, determination, and perseverance.

> Do not be frightened, daughters, by the many things you need to consider in order to begin this divine journey which is the royal road to heaven. A great treasure is gained by traveling this road; no wonder we have to pay what seems to us a high price. The time will come when you will understand how trifling everything is next to so precious a reward.

Now returning to those who want to journey on this road and continue until they reach the end, which is to drink from this water of life, I say that how they are to begin is very important—in fact, all important. They must have a great and very resolute determination to persevere until reaching the end, come what may, happen what may, whatever work is involved, whatever criticism arises, whether they arrive or whether they die on the road, or even if they don't have courage for the trials that are met, or if the whole world collapses (21.1–2).

But not only must discouragement, desolation, and depression be combated: so too must other temptations of the devil such as distractions and deception (20.4; 21.6–9). On the way of prayer, however, there is an incomparable companion, guide, and friend: Christ himself (26.1). The way along which Christ leads Teresa and her nuns is none other than that of his own cross:[12]

Take up that cross, daughters. Don't mind at all if the Jews trample upon you, if His trial can thereby be lessened. Pay no attention to what they say to you, be deaf to their gossip. In stumbling, in falling with your Spouse, do not withdraw from the cross or abandon it. Consider carefully the fatigue with which He walks and how much greater His trials are than those trials you suffer, however great you may want to paint them and no matter how much you grieve over them. You will come out consoled because you will see that they are something to be laughed at when compared to those of the Lord (26.7).

Chapters 27–42: Ascent to the Higher World of Heaven

"[Wherever] God is, there is heaven" (28.2).

Although in chapters 16–26 Teresa stresses that the path of prayer leads to heaven, the "haven of light" (19.1) and the "heavenly fount . . . of . . . living water" (19.14),[13] the image of the road/way/path clearly predominates. By contrast, in chapters 27–42 the image of heaven prevails. In the *Life*, once Teresa began to follow resolutely the "path of prayer" (*Life,* 11.1), she became the recipient of supernatural favors and forms of prayer associated with the earthly paradise and heaven (*Life*, chapters 11–29 and 37–40). Consonant with this movement in her own spiritual development, Teresa presents a commentary on the Lord's Prayer in chapters 27–42 of the *Way* in which she teaches at length about the prayer of recollection, prayer of quiet, and the reception of the Eucharist, each of which the saint links to the higher world of heaven. Thus in this final section of the *Way*, the accent falls on the ascent of the soul to heaven through prayer.

The earthly paradise and heaven are levels of the mythological universe upon which Frye's theory of descents and ascents is based (see *Secular Scripture*, 97–98). Sometimes these levels are not only external but internal. For example, in the *Life* the exterior earthly paradise of St. Joseph's monastery (chapter 35) is paralleled by the interior one of Teresa's soul (chapters 11–22).[14] Similarly, in the *Way* as well as in the *Interior Castle*, Teresa conceives of parallel worlds of an exterior heaven and an interior heaven. As one scholar has recently observed of the soul's journey in the *Interior Castle*, "The soul simultaneously rises to the upper heavenly world as it struggles toward the interior heaven."[15] Likewise, in the *Way* the path of prayer not only leads to the upper celestial world but also to the inner heaven of the soul.

At the beginning of chapter 28, explaining the phrase of the Lord's Prayer "Who art in heaven," Teresa succinctly articulates the principle whereby the soul can become heaven: "You already know that God is everywhere. It's obvious, then, that where the king is there is his court; in sum, wherever God is, there is heaven. Without a doubt you can believe that where His Majesty is present, all glory is present" (28.1). Consequently when Teresa and her nuns practice the prayer of recollection, whereby "the soul collects its faculties together and enters within itself to be with its God" (28.4), they can enclose themselves "within this little heaven of our soul, where the Maker of heaven and earth is present" (28.5). Teresa also refers to the soul in this state as a paradise (29.4). Moreover, often the soul that becomes heaven or paradise is simultaneously a castle or palace (28.6, 9, 11–12).

The prayer of quiet is distinct from the prayer of recollection because the former, unlike the latter, is a supernatural form of prayer that cannot be acquired by human effort (31.6). Nonetheless, the prayer of quiet also transforms the soul into heaven. In this prayer the Lord "places the kingdom of heaven in the soul's house" (31.11) in order to give it "a clear foretaste of what will be given to those He brings to His kingdom" (30.6). Teresa describes the kingdom of heaven as follows:

> Now, then, the great good that it seems to me there will be in the kingdom of heaven, among many other blessings, is that one will no longer take any account of earthly things, but have a calmness and glory within, rejoice in the fact that all are rejoicing, experience perpetual peace

and a wonderful inner satisfaction that comes from seeing that everyone hallows and praises the Lord and blesses His name and that no one offends Him. Everyone loves Him there, and the soul itself doesn't think about anything else than loving Him; nor can it cease loving Him, because it knows Him. And would that we could love Him in this way here below, even though we may not be able to do so with such perfection or stability. But if we knew Him we would love in a way very different from that in which we do love Him (30.5).

Yet another way in which the soul becomes heaven is by the reception of Holy Communion. In the "heavenly bread" (34.5) of the Eucharist, Christ is truly present as he was when he walked on this earth (34.6):

Receiving Communion is not like picturing with the imagination, as when we reflect upon the Lord on the cross or in other episodes of the Passion, when we picture within ourselves how things happened to Him in the past. In Communion the event is happening now, and it is entirely true. There's no reason to go looking for Him in some other place farther away. Since we know that Jesus is with us as long as the natural heat doesn't consume the accidents of bread, we should approach Him. Now, then, if when He went about in the world the mere touch of His robes cured the sick, why doubt, if we have faith, that miracles will be worked while He is within us and that He will give what we ask of Him, since He is in our house? His Majesty is not accustomed to paying poorly for His lodging if the hospitality is good (34.8).

It may seem that in this final section of the *Way* we are far removed from the heroic combat with the demonic world of the other parts of the work. On the contrary, Teresa cautions her sisters throughout this section about losing the heaven they experience in their souls by succumbing to the numerous traps, tricks, and deceptions set by the devil for "those who take the path of prayer" (39.7). This is the perspective with which Teresa leaves her sisters at the end of the *Way,* as she comments on the final petitions of the Lord's Prayer, "And lead us not into temptation, but deliver us from evil." They are to be "the soldiers of Christ, those who experience contemplation and engage in prayer . . . eager to fight" (38.2) and "wage war on the world and the devils" (40.2) from the "two fortified castles" (40.2) of the love and of the fear of God.

In conclusion, the *Way* is structured and unified by a sequence of archetypes of romance that are patterned on and in continuity with those found in the *Life:* the heroic defense of identity and the earthly paradise and heaven of St. Joseph's in Ávila against the devil who seeks to enter the monastery by means of excessive love, attachments, and concern for honor and thus turn it into "a hell here on earth" (13.5); separation from the dark and labyrinthine demonic world by traveling the "royal road" (21.1) of prayer that leads to the "haven of light" (19.1) and the "heavenly fount . . . of . . . living water" (19.14); and ascent to the upper heavenly world and interior heaven of the soul by the prayer of recollection, the prayer of quiet, and the reception of the Eucharist. In the *Life* Teresa's experience becomes archetypal, because it is shaped according to the archetypes of romance. In the *Way* Teresa's experience is archetypal in a way that goes a step beyond the *Life*. The evolution of Teresa's own spiritual life as presented in the *Life* determines the shape she gives to the conventual life of the reformed Carmel, beginning with St. Joseph's in Ávila, which will serve as the prototype for her subsequent foundations.

3

The *Interior Castle*

More has been written about the *Interior Castle*, universally acknowledged as St. Teresa's masterwork, than any of her other works. Discussion of the book's coherence has focused exclusively on the allegory of the interior castle. Although traditional scholarship considers the *Castle* the most systematic and carefully planned and arranged of Teresa's books, it still evaluates somewhat negatively its unity. For instance, E. Allison Peers believed that the castle allegory gives the work "a certain unity which some of [Teresa's] other books lack," but that "the book sometimes fails to maintain its precision of method, and falls into . . . 'sweet disorder.'"[1] Helmut Hatzfeld is more unfavorable. While the *Castle* "is the most systematic work of Santa Teresa within her informal 'improvisations,'" nonetheless, "it is clear that her rambling occupies more space than her systematization."[2] In Hatzfeld's view, the castle allegory is eclipsed by secondary allegories such as those of the fountain in the fourth mansions, silkworm/butterfly in the fifth mansions, and betrothal and marriage in the sixth and seventh mansions, respectively.[3] In the same vein, according to E. W. Trueman Dicken, these secondary allegories are "in strict logic incompatible with the principal allegory of the successive chambers of the castle."[4] Similarly, Catherine Swietlicki observes that throughout the *Castle* Teresa's "line of thought frequently hops to other sets of metaphors that may seem incongruous with the central conception of seven interconnected mansions. The abrupt jumps to other symbol systems lend an Alice-in-Wonderland quality to the work."[5] Finally, for Ángel Raimundo Fernández, the castle allegory structures the first through fifth mansions, but is diffused in the sixth and seventh mansions by the allegories of betrothal and marriage and by the images of light, fire, and water.[6]

During the past decade several scholars have evaluated the *Castle's* unity more favorably. Víctor García de la Concha asserts that the structure of the *Castle* is flexible but not disordered. The work is structured by the nuclear simile of the interior castle that Teresa develops into an allegory that in turn generates a network of similes that simultaneously remain part of the larger allegory as well as develop into secondary allegories.[7] Juan Fernández Jiménez contends that the castle allegory is clearly present throughout the *Castle*, and that the secondary allegories of the silkworm/butterfly and betrothal and marriage do not detract from the principal allegory but are in complete harmony with it.[8] E. Michael Gerli maintains that Teresa deliberately and exactly constructs the castle allegory according to the rules of the medieval and Renaissance art of memory in order to teach and disseminate her spiritual doctrine at a time when opposition to her reform was most intense; hence, the *Castle* is a coherent, complex, and sophisticated work of literary and religious art.[9] Alison Weber regards the *Castle's* structure and coherence as intentionally elusive. Teresa purposely accumulates and mixes competing and conflicting allegories and images in order to draw attention away from the later mansions' erotic nuptial mysticism that would have been dangerous in Counter-Reformation Spain because of the close link between ecstasy and the heresy of sexual impeccability in Illuminism.[10]

As we have seen in the preceding chapters, when the *Life* and the *Way of Perfection*, generally deemed to lack narrative unity, are read with the aid of Frye's grammar of narrative, they reveal a remarkable narrative unity. The *Castle* also displays an obvious narrative unity when approached from the perspective of romance. Moreover, this approach resolves the scholarly debate over the relationship between the central castle allegory and secondary allegories, since in the archetypal universe of romance the castle, fountain, butterfly, and betrothal and marriage are all either images of ascent or of ideal higher worlds. Thus, romance not only offers a new way of finding a unity in the *Castle* but also moves scholarly discussion of this question onto new ground.

In the *Life* Teresa charts for her confessors and spiritual directors the course of her spiritual development up to 1565. In the *Way* she sets forth, for the instruction of the nuns at St. Joseph's, her ideal of Carmelite community life, an ideal shaped and determined by the evolution of Teresa's own spiritual life as recounted earlier in the *Life*. In the *Castle* the saint maps out, for her sisters at St. Joseph's and the ten other reformed monasteries she had founded up to 1577, a plan of individual spiritual development that is based on her own experience and the communal Carmelite ideal.

In this chapter we will discover that in the *Castle* the archetypal world of the *Life* and the *Way* continues to be developed. In the *Life* before Teresa could restore the earthly paradise of the monastery, she first had to restore the paradise of her own soul. So, too, before the castle/ monastery of the *Way* can serve as an effective defense against the devil and his henchmen—the enemies of the Church and Teresa's reform—the soul of each individual nun in the monastery must be a castle that is secured from within. The *Castle* tells the story of this process of individual spiritual development. The story is shaped by some of the same or variations on the archetypes of romance that are outstanding in the *Life* and the *Way*. First, the soul becomes conscious of its own identity. It has a supernatural origin and destiny, for it is made in God's image and likeness and for friendship with him. Next, the soul receives "calls" from the Lord to ascend to him by withdrawing and detaching itself from the loathsome animals of the demonic world, that is, worldly business and pleasures that inhabit the outer reaches of the castle and inhibit its movement toward God. But to proceed on its ascent, the soul must overcome various obstacles. It must engage in constant combat with the demonic world, which contests every step of its progress, and surrender itself completely to God's will. This surrender is prerequisite for the soul's ascent through the various levels of its interior heaven until it reaches the inner sanctum of the seventh mansions, where it is happily and inseparably joined with God.

1st Mansions: Remembrance of Real Identity

"[We] seldom consider the precious things that can be found in this soul, or who dwells within it, or its high value" (1.1.2).

In romance the hero is frequently accompanied by animals in his or her descent into the dark and labyrinthine demonic night world, where he or she is often not only surrounded by animal shapes but also identified with animals (*Secular Scripture*, 105, 111, 115). By contrast, in ascent the hero casts off whatever conceals or frustrates identity and progresses from darkness to light (*Secular Scripture*, 133–34, 140). Frye further specifies: "In traditional romance, including Dante, the upward journey is the journey of a creature returning to its creator" (*Secular Scripture*, 157).

The primary narrative movement of the *Castle* is the soul's gradual and progressive ascent from the dark and reptile-infested outer courtyard of the castle to the luminous seventh mansions. Here can be found God the Sun who illuminates the other six mansions, with the light decreasing in intensity as the distance increases from the innermost chamber.[11] (God remains at the center of the soul even if it be in mortal sin, although his light has no effect on the soul because a black cloth or pitch covers it [see 1.2.3–4].) Paradoxically, this upward movement (ascent) is also an inward movement (descent, but not in Frye's sense of a descent into hell), since the soul itself is the interior castle of seven mansions and the seventh is "in the center and middle" of the soul (1.1.3; cf. 2.1.11). Nonetheless, Teresa most often refers to the soul's movement through the various mansions as an ascent.[12]

For Teresa, the upward journey of the soul to its God begins with the soul's remembrance of its true identity, just as in romance the hero's recollection of individual identity enables him or her to ascend to higher worlds (*Secular Scripture*, 129, 156–57). The fundamental identity of the soul is that it is created in the image and likeness of God himself (1.1.1); hence, it possesses "magnificent beauty" and the "marvelous capacity" for friendship with God (1.1.1). Beautiful shining crystal castles and palaces are a regular feature of the landscape of the romances of chivalry such as *Amadís de Gaula*, which is the most famous of the Spanish chivalric romances and which, it is believed, Teresa read. In fact, several distinguished scholars have suggested that these romances, and perhaps *Amadís* in particular, may have even inspired Teresa, for she envisions the beauty of the soul as "a castle made entirely out of a diamond or of very clear crystal, in which there are many rooms, just as in heaven there are many dwelling places" (1.1.1).[13] The soul is simultaneously a "paradise where the Lord says He finds His delight" (1.1.1); a "pearl from the Orient" (1.2.1); a "tree of life planted in the very living waters of life—that is, in God" (1.2.1); and a "heavenly interior building" (1.2.7; cf. 7.1.5). All of these images pertain to the higher worlds of the earthly paradise and heaven and underscore the soul's ascending movement.

The soul recovers its identity by prayer and reflection, the door of entry to the interior castle (1.1.7). It maintains its identity by self-knowledge and humility, that is, the constant awareness of God's grandeur and majesty and the soul's corresponding beauty, dignity, and creatureliness. "[We] seldom consider the precious things that can be found in this soul, or who dwells within it, or its high value. Consequently, little effort is made to preserve its beauty" (1.1.2; cf. 7.1.1). This self-knowledge is "the right road" and "safe and level path" (1.2.9) that leads to the subsequent sets of rooms of the castle. Furthermore, to enter into the second mansions, the soul must strive to free itself from the insects, vermin, snakes, vipers, and poisonous creatures that inhabit the outskirts of the castle, enter the first mansions with it, and blind it so that it cannot see the light coming from the central chamber (1.2.14). These animal companions, all of which are part of the demonic world,[14] personify the worldly possessions, concern for honor, and preoccupation with business matters that distract and absorb the soul, thus inhibiting the soul's consciousness of its identity by drawing its attention away from God and his image and presence in the soul. Teresa writes of those souls who enter the first mansions:

> For even though they are very involved in the world, they have good desires and sometimes, though only once in a while, they entrust themselves to our Lord and reflect on who they are, although in a rather hurried fashion. During the period of a month they will sometimes pray, but their minds are then filled with business matters which ordinarily occupy them. They are so attached to these things that where their treasure lies their heart goes also. Sometimes they do put all these things aside, and the self-knowledge and awareness that they are not proceeding correctly in order to get to the door is important. Finally, they enter the first, lower rooms. But so many reptiles get in with them that they are prevented from seeing the beauty of the castle

and from calming down; they have done quite a
bit just by having entered (1.1.8).

Souls that fail to struggle to free themselves from involve-
ment in external matters are not only prohibited from
entering the second mansions but are in danger of becoming like "the insects and vermin that are in the wall
surrounding the castle" (1.1.6) and "falling and carrying
on . . . like brute beasts" (1.1.7), thus entirely losing their
own identity.

At every stage of its ascent, the soul must defend its
progress against the devil. Teresa exhorts, "Remember
that there are few dwelling places in this castle in which
the devils do not wage battle. . . . It is very necessary that
we don't grow careless in recognizing the wiles of the
devil, and that he not deceive us by changing himself into
an angel of light" (1.2.15; cf. *Way of Perfection*, 38.2; 39,
passim). The saint further compares the devil to "a noise-
less file, that we need to recognize . . . at the outset"
(1.2.16). In this initial phase of ascent, the soul must be
on guard against indiscreet zeal, which causes serious
harm in monasteries, namely, "the cooling of the charity
and love the Sisters have for one another" (1.2.17). "[True]
perfection," Teresa avers, "consists in love of God and
neighbor; the more perfectly we keep these two commandments the more perfect we will be" (1.2.17).

2nd Mansions: Calls to Ascent

> "[These] persons are able to hear the Lord when He calls" (2.1.2).

It has already been mentioned in the initial chapter
of this study that in romance the hero frequently receives

a "call" that prompts him or her to recover his or her identity, escape from the lower world in which the hero is trapped or imprisoned, and ascend to higher worlds (*Secular Scripture*, 136–37, 156–57). This archetype of romance is outstanding in chapters 9–10 of the *Life*. Teresa received two "calls" that enabled her to recover her identity as the friend of God by practicing mental prayer regularly and avoiding occasions of sin, to liberate herself from the metaphorical and psychological hell in which she had been trapped for almost two decades, and to ascend to the higher worlds of the earthly paradise and heaven. This same archetype is also present in the second mansions of the *Castle*.

Souls who enter the second mansions have begun to practice prayer that makes it possible for them to recover their identity as creatures and friends of God who have a supernatural origin and destiny; however, they do not avoid the occasions of sin that, of course, threaten the very identity they have recovered. The source of these occasions of sin are "pastimes, business affairs, pleasures, and worldly buying and selling" (2.1.2). Although the soul has detached itself somewhat from these things, for example, it recognizes that they are dangerous, it has not done so completely. In the second mansions then the Lord seeks to draw the soul to himself and away from unnecessary things and business affairs. "Yet this Lord desires intensely that we love Him and seek His company, so much so that from time to time He calls us to draw near Him. And his voice is so sweet the poor soul dissolves at not doing immediately what He commands" (2.1.2). These "calls" take various forms. "[They] come through words spoken by other good people, or through sermons, or through what is read in good books, or through the many things that are heard and by which God calls, or through illnesses and trials, or also through a truth that He teaches during the brief moments we spend in prayer" (2.1.3).

Not surprisingly, the demonic world raises "an uproar" (2.1.4) against these "calls" to advance and draw closer to the Lord. The focus of this particular attack is the soul's perseverance and resolution. "It is in this stage that the devils represent these snakes (worldly things) and the temporal pleasures of the present as though almost eternal. They bring to mind the esteem one has in the world, one's friends and relatives, one's health (when there's thought of penitential practices, for the soul that enters this dwelling place always begins wanting to practice some penance) and a thousand other obstacles" (2.1.3). The greater the soul's determination and capacity for advancement, the more ferocious will be the devil's assaults. "[He] will gather all hell together to make the soul go back outside [the castle]" (2.1.5). The soul's weapons in this warfare are constant awareness "how all its good is within this castle" (2.1.6); withdrawal from bad companions; conversation with souls who are in this mansion and, most especially, "those known to have entered the ones closer to the center" (2.1.6); and strong determination "not to be conquered" and "to fight with all the devils" (2.1.6), to be faithful to prayer, and to make "every possible effort to bring [its] will into conformity with God's will" (2.1.8), since God permits these assaults in order to test the soul's stability. The soul will never find peace and rest outside itself if it does not obtain and have them in its own house (2.1.9). The soul cannot attain heaven without entering itself. "[It] is foolish to think that we will enter heaven without entering into ourselves, coming to know ourselves, reflecting on our misery and what we owe God, and begging Him often for mercy" (2.1.11). The soul that perseveres in the face of these trials will advance, and God will give it dominion over the "wild animals," that is, the pastimes and business matters that gave it so much trouble in these mansions. "Let [these souls] trust in the mercy of God and not at all in themselves, and they will see how His Majesty brings them from the dwelling places of one stage to those of another and settles them in a land where these wild animals cannot touch or tire them, but where they themselves will bring all these animals into subjection and scoff at them" (2.1.9). As noted in the exposition of the archetypal world of romance in the first chapter of this study, wild animals pertain to the demonic world. Consequently, the dominion over wild animals that God gives the soul connotes a return (ascent) to the earthly paradise, where humanity lived in harmony with the animals that inhabited Eden and in intimacy with God.[15]

| 3rd Mansions: Conquest of Obstacles to Ascent | "[When] it seems [these souls] have become lords of the world. . . . His Majesty will try them in some minor matters" (3.2.1). |

To ascend from the night world, the hero of romance must often overcome a series of obstacles, "adventures which involve separation, loneliness, humiliation, pain, and the threat of more pain" (*Secular Scripture*, 53; cf. 26,

67). Hence, among the forms that heroism takes in romance are suffering, endurance, and patience. This is specifically "the ethos of the Christian myth, where the heroism of Christ takes the form of enduring the Passion" (*Secular Scripture*, 88).

The souls who enter the third mansions have won—"through perseverance and the mercy of God" (3.1.1)—the battles of the second mansions. Thus, they have demonstrated their heroism by defending their identity and spiritual progress against the fierce assaults of the demonic world and by patiently enduring much suffering in the process. However, to advance further into the castle, these souls must overcome yet more obstacles that entail pain and suffering.

The hallmark of the souls who enter the third mansions is a well-ordered life. Teresa describes them as follows: "They long not to offend His Majesty, even guarding themselves against venial sins; they are fond of doing penance and setting aside periods for recollection; they spend their time well, practicing works of charity toward their neighbors; and are very balanced in their use of speech and dress and in the governing of their households—those who have them" (3.1.5). The well-balanced life of the souls who are in the third mansions is both a strength and a weakness. It is an asset because it has enabled them to enter these mansions; it is a liability because it is an obstacle for them to progress further. The main obstacle to be overcome in the third mansions is reason, for the soul is now challenged to allow the love of God to overwhelm reason. Teresa puts it this way:

> The penance these souls do is well balanced, like their lives. They desire penance a great deal so as

to serve our Lord by it. Nothing of this is wrong,
and thus they are very discreet in doing it in a
way so as not to harm their health. Have no
fear that they will kill themselves, for their reason is still very much in control. Love has not
yet reached the point of overwhelming reason.
But I should like us to use our reason to make
ourselves dissatisfied with this way of serving
God, always going step by step, for we'll never
finish this journey. . . . Let us exert ourselves, my
Sisters, for the love of the Lord; let's abandon
our reason and our fears into His hands; let's
forget this natural weakness that can take up our
attention so much. . . . As for ourselves, we
should care only about moving quickly so as to
see this Lord (3.2.7–8).

The soul then must surrender the control and direction of its life entirely to God if it wants to ascend higher
and penetrate deeper inside the castle. The concrete form
this surrender takes is complete detachment from consolation in prayer and from worldly esteem and honor in
human affairs, since the Lord himself tests the souls in the
third mansions by letting them experience spiritual dry-
ness and opportunities "to be despised or to lose a little
honor" (3.2.5). The fortitude of those souls who surmount the trials of these mansions is that of "those who
are tried in suffering," are true friends of the cross, and are
able to withstand "the storms of the world" and tempests
stirred up by the devil (3.2.12; cf. 3.1.9).

Mansions 4–7:
Ascent Heavenward

"[Since] in some way we can enjoy heaven on earth, be brave in begging the Lord to give us His grace in such a way that nothing will be lacking through our own fault" (5.1.2).

In the *Life*, once Teresa entrusted the course of her life to God, her life began an ascending movement. God granted her supernatural favors and forms of prayer that transported her to the higher worlds of the earthly paradise and heaven and drew her into closer intimacy with him. Similarly, the souls who enter the fourth mansions are those who have overcome reason, who do not "think much but . . . love much" (4.1.7), and who have surrendered totally to God. Beginning in these mansions and continuing in the subsequent ones, God will grant these souls supernatural favors and forms of prayer that will transport them in ascending stages to the higher world of heaven that is simultaneously above and at the center of the soul. Moreover, at each stage the soul must defend its ascent against the demonic world.

From the outset of the *Castle*, it is clear that the interior castle is by its nature part of the higher world of heaven, for in it "there are many rooms, just as in heaven there are many dwelling places" (1.1.1) and in its center "is the room or royal chamber where the King [God] stays" (1.2.8). Indeed, the castle is a "heavenly interior building" (1.2.7), because, as Teresa stated in the *Way of Perfection*, "wherever God is, there is heaven" (*Way*, 28.1). It is also a paradise (1.1.1) in which the "tree of life [is] planted in the very living waters of life" (1.2.1), because God's presence makes it so, just as his presence made Eden the earthly paradise and makes heaven paradise. Additionally, it is a "pearl from the Orient" (1.2.1), because the kingdom of heaven is like a pearl of great price (see Matt. 13.45–46). The images Teresa employs to explain the supernatural favors and forms of prayer God bestows upon the soul in the fourth through seventh mansions—the fountain, silkworm/butterfly, and betrothal and marriage—pertain to the same higher world of heaven, as does the interior castle, and bring to the fore other aspects of the castle's celestial nature.

In the fourth mansions the soul is granted the supernatural prayer of spiritual delight (or quiet, as Teresa calls it in the *Life,* chapters 14–15) as well as that of recollection. In the prayer of recollection, God gently draws the soul and its faculties, even if they have wandered outside the castle, inward to himself in the soul, which is an interior heaven because of God's presence therein. To explain this prayer, Teresa uses the image of the Good Shepherd, a major archetype of the higher worlds (*Anatomy of Criticism,* 141–34; *Great Code,* 142; cf. *Secular Scripture,* 100–101). "Like a good shepherd, with a whistle so gentle that even [the faculties] themselves almost fail to hear it, He makes them recognize His voice and stops them from going so far astray so that they will return to their dwelling place. And this shepherd's whistle has such power that they abandon the exterior things in which they were estranged from Him and enter the castle" (4.3.2). This supernatural prayer of recollection is distinct from the recollection discussed in the *Way of Perfection.* The latter can be achieved with the help of God's grace through human effort, whereas the soul can do nothing to acquire the former since it is a divine favor.

Spiritual delight is also a favor granted only by God and is different from the spiritual consolation the soul experiences in meditation. In order to explain this distinction, Teresa uses the comparison of how the basins or troughs of two fountains are filled with water in different ways. One is filled with water that comes from "far away through many aqueducts and the use of much ingenuity" (4.2.3); this is comparable to "consolations . . . that are drawn from meditation" since they come "through our own efforts" (4.2.3). By contrast, "with the other the source of the water is right there, and the trough fills without any noise. There is no need of any skill, nor does the building of aqueducts have to continue; but water is always flowing from the spring" (4.2.3); this refers to spiritual delight since "with this . . . fount, the water comes from its own source which is God" (4.2.4). The image of the fountain, with abundant and overflowing water (4.2.3), makes clear not only the supernatural nature of spiritual delight but also that this divine favor connotes an ascent to higher worlds, for the fountain is an element of the landscape of both the earthly paradise and heaven.[16]

In the fifth mansions the soul "can enjoy heaven on earth," the hidden treasure that lies within it (5.1.2), in a way that surpasses its experience in the fourth mansions. God grants the soul the prayer of union. "This union is above all earthly joys, above all delights, above all consolations, and still more than that" (5.1.6). In this favor the Lord enters "the center of the soul without going through any door, as He entered the place where His disciples were when He said *pax vobis* ['peace be with you']; or as He left the tomb without lifting away the stone" (5.1.12). The Lord then "so places Himself in the interior of that soul that when it returns to itself it can in no way doubt that it was in God and God was in it" (5.1.9). The essence and enduring effect of this experience is a union of wills between God and the soul. Teresa images this union by the comparison of the silkworm/butterfly. The silkworm constructs a cocoon, dies, and emerges from the cocoon as a beautiful white butterfly. Apropos of this comparison, Teresa comments:

> Therefore, courage, my daughters! Let's be quick to do this work and weave this little cocoon by getting rid of our self-love and self-will, our attachment to any earthly thing, and by performing deeds of penance, prayer, mortification, obedience, and of all the other things you know. . . . Let it die; let this silkworm die, as it does in completing what it was created to do! And you will see how we see God, as well as ourselves placed inside His greatness, as is this little silkworm within its cocoon. . . .

> Now, then, let's see what this silkworm does, for that's the reason I've said everything else. When the soul is, in this prayer, truly dead to the world, a little white butterfly comes forth. Oh, greatness of God! How transformed the soul is when it comes out of this prayer after having been placed within the greatness of God and so closely joined with Him for a little while—in my opinion the union never lasts for as much as a half hour. Truly, I tell you that the soul doesn't recognize itself. Look at the difference there is between an ugly worm and a little white butterfly; that's what the difference is here (5.2.6–7).

The image of the silkworm/butterfly is one of rebirth, resurrection, new life, and ascent from the night world of darkness and death. The cocoon is a totally dark condition for the silkworm. It is simultaneously a dark sepulcher and an incubator sustaining life. The literal darkness of the cocoon parallels the "dark interval" that the soul experiences when, during the process of bringing itself into conformity with God's will, its own will is challenged and broken. But out of this dark disorientation and confusion emerges a new life in which the center of gravity has been shifted from self to God.[17] The silkworm/butterfly comparison is a retelling of the story of descent and ascent that is the prototype of Christian romance: Christ's death and resurrection (see *Great Code*, 174–75; *Secular Scripture*, 163) that "includes the invitation to enter into the dying and rising of Christ and so enter into union with God."[18] Moreover, the butterfly (*mariposa*) or dove (*paloma*), as Teresa also calls it (in sixteenth-century as well as present-day Spanish, *mariposa* and *paloma* are used synonymously), is in its own right an image of ascent since it symbolizes flight (*Secular Scripture*, 151).[19] Teresa herself emphasizes this aspect of the image at the beginning of chapter 4 of the fifth mansions. "It seems to me you have a desire to see what this little dove is doing and where it rests since as was explained [in the preceding chapters] it rests neither in spiritual delights nor in earthly consolations. Its flight is higher, and I cannot satisfy your desire until the last dwelling place" (5.4.1).

Combat with the demonic world is an integral part of the mystical life, as Teresa knew from her own experience and as she tried to impress upon her sisters in the *Way of Perfection*. She returns to this point in the *Castle*. The growing intimacy between God and the soul that occurs in the fourth and fifth mansions is contested by the demonic world. The souls in the fourth mansions "suffer much combat" because the devil wears "himself out trying to lead the soul to perdition" (4.3.10). For this reason Teresa urges the soul to avoid occasions of sin. "I advise them so strongly not to place themselves in the occasions of sin because the devil tries much harder for a soul of this kind than for very many to whom the Lord does not grant these favors. For such a soul can do a great deal of harm to the devil by getting others to follow it, and it could be of great benefit to God's Church" (4.3.10). The soul must be equally vigilant in the fifth mansions for "[there] is no enclosure so fenced in that [the devil] cannot enter, or desert so withdrawn that he fails to go there" (5.4.8). Although in these mansions the soul is attached to God's will, the devil attempts to deceive the soul. "[Under] the color of good, [the devil] confuses it with regard to little things and induces it to get taken up with some of them that he makes it think are good. Then little by little he darkens the intellect, cools the will's ardor, and makes self-love grow until in one way or another he withdraws the soul from the will of God and brings it to his own" (5.4.8).

The prayer of union, which is no more than a brief meeting between God and the soul, is a prelude to the spiritual betrothal of the sixth mansions. As the soul enters these mansions, it is anxious that this betrothal take place; however, God wants the soul to desire this betrothal even more so that it takes place at a cost. Consequently, the soul will suffer severe interior and exterior trials as well as enjoy greater favors, all of which are associated with heaven. Among the obstacles the soul must surmount in its ascent in the sixth mansions are ridicule and praise by others, the severest illnesses, inexperienced confessors, the inability to explain itself and the resultant feeling it has deceived its confessors, and interior oppression by the devil comparable "to the oppression of those that suffer in hell, for no consolation is allowed in the midst of this tempest" (6.1.9). The soul's guide and model in these tribulations, as in all of life's trials, is "the good Jesus" (6.7.6). "Life is long, and there are in it many trials, and we need to look at Christ our model, how He suffered them, and also at His apostles and saints, so as to bear these trials with perfection" (6.7.13). The heroism that the soul manifests in overcoming these obstacles to its continuing ascent then is a sharing in the heroism of Christ himself in his Passion (see *Secular Scripture*, 88).

God not only tests and purifies the soul by trials in the sixth mansions, he also bestows favors on it. For example, God sends the soul raptures, in which he shows it "some secrets, things about heaven" (6.4.5) and places it "in this room of the empyreal heaven that we must have interiorly. For clearly, the soul has some of these dwelling places since God abides within it" (6.4.8). In another kind of rapture, flight of the spirit, the soul is transported to "another region different from this in which we live, where there is shown another light so different from earth's light" (6.5.7). The soul is also granted imaginative visions of the saints in heaven and intellectual visions of "a multitude of angels with their Lord" (6.5.8). The purpose of these celestial favors, "the jewels the Spouse begins to give the betrothed" (6.5.11), is "to show [the soul] something about its future land so that it may suffer the trials of this laborious path" (6.5.9)[20] and to increase even more its desire to be united inseparably with the Lord.

In romance, virginity or spiritual marriage represents a return to higher worlds (*Secular Scripture*, 84; cf. 54).

Appropriately, therefore, the spiritual marriage between God and the soul takes place in God's own dwelling place in the seventh mansions, that is, in the heaven within the soul:

> When our Lord is pleased to have pity on this soul that He has already taken spiritually as His Spouse because of what it suffers and has suffered through its desires, He brings it, before the spiritual marriage is consummated, into His dwelling place which is this seventh. For just as in heaven so in the soul His Majesty must have a room where He dwells alone. Let us call it another heaven. . . . The Lord puts the soul in this dwelling place of His, which is the center of the soul itself. They say that the empyreal heaven where the Lord is does not move as do the other heavens; similarly, it seems, in the soul that enters here there are none of those movements that usually take place in the faculties and the imagination and do harm to the soul, nor do these stirrings take away its peace (7.1.3, 2.9).

While in the fifth and sixth mansions the soul's union with God is momentary, in the seventh mansions of the spiritual marriage the soul is permanently united with God, never to be separated from him. "So in this temple of God, in this His dwelling place, He alone and the soul rejoice together in the deepest silence" (7.3.11).[21] The soul never moves from these rooms, where God reveals to it "the glory of heaven" (7.2.3). Moreover, at the beginning of the celebration of the spiritual marriage, the soul is given an intellectual vision of the Blessed Trinity:

When the soul is brought into [this seventh] dwelling place, the Most Blessed Trinity, all three Persons, through an intellectual vision, is revealed to it through a certain representation of the truth. First there comes an enkindling in the spirit in the manner of a cloud of magnificent splendor; and these Persons are distinct, and through an admirable knowledge the soul understands as a most profound truth that all three Persons are one substance and one power and one knowledge and one God alone. It knows in such a way that what we hold by faith, it understands, we can say, through sight—although the sight is not with the bodily eyes nor with the eyes of the soul, because we are not dealing with an imaginative vision. Here all three Persons communicate themselves to it, speak to it, and explain those words of the Lord in the Gospel: that He and the Father and the Holy Spirit will come to dwell with the soul that loves Him and keeps His commandments (7.1.6).

The soul is also granted an imaginative vision of the risen Christ:

His Majesty desires to show Himself to the soul through an imaginative vision of His most sacred humanity so that the soul will understand and not be ignorant of receiving this sovereign gift. With other persons the favor will be received in another form. With regard to the one of whom we are speaking [Teresa herself], the Lord represented Himself to her, just after she had received Communion, in the form of shining

splendor, beauty, and majesty, as He was after
His resurrection, and told her that now it was
time that she consider as her own what be-
longed to Him and that He would take care of
what was hers, and He spoke other words destined more to be heard than to be mentioned
(7.2.6).

But the soul is not idle in these mansions. "All its concern
is taken up with how to please [the Lord] more and how
or where it will show Him the love it bears Him. This is
the reason for prayer, my daughters, the purpose of this
spiritual marriage: the birth always of good works, good
works" (7.4.6). The soul also endures trials and suffering.
Teresa puts it this way: "I hold for certain that these favors
are meant to fortify our weakness . . . that we may be able
to imitate [Christ] in His great sufferings. We have always
seen that those who were closest to Christ our Lord were
those with the greatest trials. Let us look at what His glorious Mother suffered and the glorious apostles" (7.4.4–5).
Thus, the ubiquitous spiritual combat is an integral part
even of the seventh mansions. "[The] calm these souls
have interiorly is for the sake of their having much less
calm exteriorly and much less desire to have exterior
calm" (7.4.10). Since "the faculties, senses, and all the
corporeal will not be idle, the soul wages more war from
the center than it did when it was outside suffering with
them, for then it didn't understand the tremendous gain
trials bring" (7.4.10).[22]

In summary, Teresa's presentation in the *Castle* of
the evolution of the spiritual life from its beginnings
through the spiritual marriage is a sequence of the archetypes of romance: the remembrance of real identity, call
to ascent, conquest of the obstacles to ascent, and ascent

to the higher world of heaven. Consequently, the *Castle* has a strong narrative unity. Moreover, the images of the fountain, silkworm/butterfly, and betrothal and marriage, which scholars have sometimes considered to supplant the castle image, are, like the castle, part of the higher world of heaven and serve to highlight various aspects of the celestial nature of the interior castle of the soul. Hence, these images are fully integrated into the *Castle's* narrative, thus also underscoring the work's internal coherence.

4

The *Foundations*

If the *Interior Castle* is the most studied of St. Teresa's four major prose works, the *Foundations* is the least. In fact, E. Allison Peers once remarked that "It must be owned that, if one of the Saint's major works had to be sacrificed—an idea at which good Teresans will very properly be horrified—it is with the *Foundations* that we should reluctantly have to part."[1]

The narrative and thematic unity of the *Foundations*—which consists of an account of Teresa's foundations of monasteries subsequent to that of St. Joseph's in Ávila, counsels to prioresses regarding a number of matters, and biographical sketches of several early discalced Carmelite nuns and friars—has been evaluated variously by scholars. It is not surprising, in view of Peers's observation, that he deems the *Foundations* "[from] the literary standpoint . . . the least commendable" of Teresa's major works, because "it rambles to excess" and is interrupted by numerous digressions, that is, the counsels to prioresses and biographical sketches.[2] For Teófanes Egido, the *Foundations* is a composite of historical and didactic elements. It offers a chronicle of Teresa's foundations as well as her teaching on diverse aspects of conventual life, often illustrated by the biographies of early Carmelites. This dual character of the *Foundations*, Egido demonstrates, is observable not only in its overall structure but sometimes within the parameters of a single chapter, for example, chapters 10, 18, and 20.[3] The different sections of the *Foundations* were written at various times. For this reason, Guido Mancini considers its structure to be tripartite: part one (chapters 1–20) was written during 1573–74; part two (chapters 21–27), in 1576; and part three (chapters 28–31), during 1580–82.[4] According to Víctor García de la Concha, the *Foundations* is structured by the story of the contest between God and the devil to win souls that turns on the axis of Teresa's obedience.[5] Finally, Alison Weber maintains that the *Foundations* is a combination of picaresque and exemplary history. The *picaresque*, a term that Weber uses synonymously with *humorous*, is evident in Teresa's story of how in making her foundations she charmingly and ingeniously outwits civil and ecclesiastical authority to accomplish her divine mission; the exemplary is represented by the interpolated tales about Teresa's nuns and her advice to prioresses.[6]

In this chapter we will find that the archetypal universe of the *Life*, the *Way of Perfection*, and the *Interior Castle* also frames the action of the *Foundations*, which tells the story of how Teresa and her nuns disseminate the earthly paradise of St. Joseph's monastery by founding other monasteries modeled on this prototype. If Teresa and her nuns are to be successful in restoring the earthly paradise that enables them to ascend to heaven in the hereafter, they must accomplish the travail of total surrender and obedience to God. Consequently, they again find themselves intensely engaged in the war between the higher and demonic worlds. In this conflict, Teresa and her nuns become angels who inhabit the restored earthly paradise of the monastery and do all they can to thwart the demonic world's efforts to prevent the dissemination of Teresa's reform and to sabotage it from within.

The archetypes of romance unify the *Foundations*, just as they do the *Life*, the *Way of Perfection*, and the *Interior Castle,* but in a somewhat different way. The archetypes of the restoration of the earthly paradise of the monastery, the heroic defense of this paradise against the demonic world, and the ascent to heaven are present in the *Foundations*, but they are not found in consecutive order as they are in Teresa's other three works. They are in evidence throughout the work and are not confined to a single chapter or group of chapters. As we will see, these archetypes are as discernible in Teresa's account of her foundations as in her counsels to prioresses and her biographies of early Carmelites, thus giving the *Foundations* the thematic and narrative unity that it seems to lack.

The Ascent to Heaven: "In obedience lies security against that dread . . . that we might stray from the path to heaven" (Prologue 1).

In the first chapter of the *Life*, the goal of the heroic quest of Teresa, the friend of God, is revealed: heaven. In the initial chapter of the *Way*, Teresa makes it clear that her Carmelite nuns are to share her fundamental identity as the friend of God and hence the object of her heroic quest: heaven. In her *Spiritual Testimonies,* Teresa reports that on February 9, 1570, the Thursday after Ash Wednesday, while she was visiting the Carmel of Malagón that she had founded two years earlier, the Lord appeared to her in an imaginative vision immediately after she received Communion, encouraging her to make more foundations and commanding her to write their history.[7] Consequently, the *Foundations* is, as Bede Edwards has pointed out, "the only one of Teresa's major works to have been written in compliance with a direct order from heaven."[8] Moreover, heaven is in the foreground at the outset of the *Foundations.* In the prologue, it is made clear that heaven is the goal of Teresa and her nuns. "In obedience lies security against that dread (which for us as mortals living in this life is a good thing) that we might stray from the path to heaven" (1).

García de la Concha has rightly emphasized the primacy of the theme of obedience in the *Foundations.*[9] Indeed, for Teresa obedience guarantees that she and her sisters are on the road to heaven. Teresa's own obedience to God brings into existence the environment that is most propitious to her and her nuns attaining heaven: the enclosed monastery, where the primitive Carmelite rule of poverty, prayer, and solitude is lived, and an apostolate of prayer for God's Church in its hour of need is carried out. God himself directs Teresa in establishing each of her foundations, from the initial inspiration to securing housing to the arrangement of the smallest details.[10] Teresa expresses it this way:

> Oh, God help me, how many obstacles I have seen in these business matters that seemed impossible to overcome, and how easy it was for

His Majesty to remove them. And how ashamed
I am not to be better after seeing what I have
seen. For now as I am writing, I am growing
fearful and want our Lord to make known to
everyone how in these foundations we creatures
have done next to nothing. The Lord has directed all by means of such lowly beginnings
that only His Majesty could have raised the work
to what it now is (13.7).

The prioress at Valladolid assisted me as much as
she could because she greatly desired the foundation of Palencia. But since she saw me so
lukewarm about it, she too was afraid. Now let
the true ardor come, for neither the nations nor
the servants of God suffice! Therefore, it is often
made clear that it is not I who do anything in
these foundations, but the work is His who is all
powerful in everything (29.5).

In the *Life*, once Teresa gives control of her life over to
God after her conversion experience, her life commences
a dramatic ascending movement. Similarly, in the third
mansions of the *Interior Castle*, Teresa avers that if the soul
wants to ascend higher and penetrate deeper into the
castle, it must surrender the control and direction of its
life entirely to God. In the *Foundations* Teresa equates this
surrender with obedience. "Those who practice obedience
remember that they resolutely surrendered their own will
to God's will, using submission to the one who stands in
God's place as a means to this surrender" (Prologue 1).
The challenge of obedience that Teresa faces in the *Foundations* is to overcome her fears, cowardice, and pusilla-

nimity (see 2.7), and to trust completely in the promise the Lord made to her when she felt powerless to help bring souls to him. "'Wait a little, daughter, and you will see great things'" (1.8). The fruit of Teresa's surrender to this promise was her foundation of more than a dozen monasteries of the reformed Carmel of her nuns and of the discalced friars. In Genesis, humanity lost Eden because of its disobedience to God's will and word; in the *Foundations,* Teresa recovers the earthly paradise by her obedience to God's will and word, an idea to which we will return shortly.

As in the *Way of Perfection,* the image of the road in the *Foundations* is one of ascent to the higher world of heaven. In the *Way* the road was that of prayer; in the *Foundations,* although Teresa refers to the path of prayer (4.3), poverty and humility (14.4), and the rule and constitutions (18.6–7), she is concerned principally with obedience. The path of obedience that leads to heaven is none other than that of Jesus Christ and his cross. "And in matters touching on obedience [the Lord] doesn't want the soul who truly loves Him to take any other path than the one He did: *obediens usque ad mortem* ['becoming obedient to death']" (5.3). This path, which is sure and leads quickly to the highest perfection (see 5.10–11), involves suffering, as it did for Teresa herself, who not only had to endure civil and ecclesiastical opposition to her foundations but hardships in traveling:

> I am not recording in these foundations the great hardships endured in the traveling: the cold, the heat, the snow (once it didn't stop snowing the whole day); sometimes getting lost, and at other times, being very sick and having a

fever (for, glory to God, I usually have poor health) (18.4).

Although we hurried along on our journey, we did not reach Seville until the Thursday before Trinity Sunday, after having endured scorching heat. Even though we did not travel during siesta time, I tell you, Sisters, that since the sun was beating on the wagons, getting into them was like stepping into purgatory. Sometimes by thinking of hell, at other times by thinking that something was being done and suffered for God, those Sisters journeyed with much happiness and joy (24.6).

You have seen, daughters, that we have undergone some trials, although I believe I have written about the least part of them. For it would be tiresome if I had to describe in detail the roads, the rain and snow, and getting lost and, above all, frequently, my very poor health (27.17).

For Teresa, suffering is an integral part of the Carmelite vocation. "And the Sister that does not feel within herself this desire [to suffer in the Lord's service] should not consider herself a true discalced nun, for our desires must not be for rest but for suffering in order to imitate in something our true Spouse" (28.43). Heroism takes many forms in romance, including suffering, endurance, and patience (*Secular Scripture*, 88). Thus, the quest of Teresa and her nuns to reach heaven by walking the path of obedience, which entails suffering, is genuinely heroic.

| Restoration of the Earthly Paradise of the Monastery: | "By bringing us to such a paradise, our Lord repaid us generously for what we had suffered" (31.39). |

Peers noted that the *Life* and the *Foundations* are closely linked. "The *Foundations* continues the story of [Teresa's] career precisely where the *Life* lays it down and carries it to a point only a few months from her death."[11] Peers's observation can be further developed, for St. Joseph's monastery in Ávila, the foundation and life-style that Teresa recounts in chapters 32–36 of the *Life*, is the prototype for her subsequent foundations (see 3.18; 9.1). In chapter 35 of the *Life*, Teresa explains the essential spiritual significance of St. Joseph's in Ávila:

> O greatness of God! Often I am amazed when I consider how particularly His Majesty wanted to help me found this little dwelling corner for God. I believe this is what it is; it is an abode in which His Majesty delights, for He once said to me while I was in prayer that this house was a paradise of delight for Him. And thus it seems His Majesty has selected the souls He has brought to this monastery. I live in their company very, very much ashamed. I wouldn't have known how to desire for this purpose souls such as these; so austere, poor, and prayerful. And they bear this austerity with a joy and happiness that makes each one feel unworthy to have deserved to come to a place like this. There are some, especially, whom the Lord called out of a world of much vanity and ostentation where they could

have been satisfied in conformity with its laws.
And the Lord has so doubled their joys in this
house that they realized clearly He has given
them a hundred joys for every one they left. . . .
With others, He has changed what was good
into something better. To those who are young
He gives fortitude and knowledge so that they
are unable to desire anything else, and they
understand that to be detached from all the
things of life is to live in the greatest calm, even
in regard to earthly things. To those who are
older and have poor health He gives strength,
and He gives them the power to bear the austerity and penance the others do (35.12).

Teresa begins her explanation by praising God's magna-
nimity for the favor he has bestowed by the foundation of
St. Joseph's. Next, in continuity with the well-established
tradition of the monastic literature of the Patristic period
and the Middle Ages that considered the monastic life to
be a return to Eden,[12] Teresa identifies St. Joseph's with
the earthly paradise. St. Joseph's is a "paradise of delight"
for God because the nuns there, who seem to have
been handpicked by the Lord himself, follow the primitive Carmelite life-style of austerity, poverty, prayer,
detachment, penance, and solitude, which is extremely
pleasing to the Lord. This identification of St. Joseph's in
Ávila with the earthly paradise is paradigmatic for the
spiritual significance of Teresa's subsequent monastic foundations. Since St. Joseph's is the prototype of these foundations, what can be said of it can also be said of all her
foundations.

   Just as Teresa begins her description of St. Joseph's in
Ávila in chapter 35 of the *Life* by focusing on the favor

God has bestowed in founding this monastery, she opens the *Foundations* by proclaiming that her purpose in this work is to make known the favors God has granted Carmel in her foundations.[13] "May . . . His Majesty . . . grant me the grace to be able to recount for His glory the favors that through these foundations He has granted this order" (Prologue 3). The principal favor God grants through Teresa's foundations is that they, like St. Joseph's in Ávila, restore the earthly paradise that leads to heaven. In the *Foundations,* there are four aspects of Teresa's discussion of her foundations subsequent to St. Joseph's in Ávila that substantiate their identification with the earthly paradise.

First, one of the themes found in Patristic and medieval monastic literature is that angels populated Eden, and the monk is called to live with and to be like the angels in the earthly paradise of the monastery. This theme also suggests that the monastery is a figure of the celestial paradise.[14] In chapter 1 of the *Foundations,* Teresa characterizes her nuns at St. Joseph's in Ávila, which was a "paradise of delight" for the Lord (*Life*, 35.12), as "angelic souls":

> Well now, this wretched one [Teresa herself] was among these angelic souls. They didn't seem to me to be anything else, for there was no fault they hid from me, even if interior. And the favors, and ardent desires, and detachment the Lord gave them were great. Their consolation was their solitude. They assured me that they never tired of being alone, and thus they felt it a torment when others came to visit them, even if these were their brothers. The one who had the greater opportunity to remain in a hermitage considered herself the luckiest. In considering

the real value of these souls and the courage God
gave them to serve and suffer for Him, certainly
not a characteristic of women, I often thought
that the riches God placed in them were meant
for some great purpose (1.6).

Subsequently, she speaks of nuns who died in her monasteries as being angelic at the hour of death, highlighting
her foundations' paradisal quality, which prefigures the
ultimate paradise of heaven. Beatriz de la Encarnación of
the Valladolid Carmel died with "her eyes fixed on heaven
. . . looking like an angel" (12.8), while an unnamed sister
of St. Joseph's monastery in Toledo died "like an angel"
(16.4).[15] Teresa's identification of her nuns with angels is
corroborated by Fray Luis de León, the leading Spanish
biblical exegete of the day, who was selected to prepare
the first edition of the saint's works published in 1588.
Addressing the Mother Prioress Ana de Jesús and the nuns
of the Madrid Carmel, the Augustinian friar writes in the
dedicatory letter to his edition, "For there is no lady in the
world who takes such pleasure in her own adornment as
do Your Reverences in living like angels. And angels you
certainly are, not only in perfection of life but also in the
similarity and the unity that exists between you."[16]

   Second, Teresa states that her monastery at Burgos is
a paradise, due to its garden and view. "By bringing us to
such a paradise, our Lord repaid us generously for what
we had suffered. Because of the garden, the view, and the
water, the property is nothing else but that" (31.39).
Actual monastic gardens reinforced the metaphor of the
earthly paradise of the monastery.[17] For Teresa, the garden was an essential element of the monastery, thus
casting into relief its paradisal nature. As Kieran Kavanaugh
has pointed out, "If elaborate or expensive architecture

elicited a frown from Teresa as far as her ideals were concerned, a beautiful view and a garden with trees and flowers were all-important to her. The garden, as well, served as a place for hermitages. In St. Joseph's in Ávila as many as ten hermitages were put up in the garden while Teresa was living there."[18]

Third, St. Joseph's in Ávila was a "paradise of delight" for God because of the virtuous living of the nuns with whom he peopled the monastery. In the *Foundations* Teresa testifies that the Lord has filled her foundations with souls who excel in the virtues first practiced at St. Joseph's (see 9.1; 12.10; 16.1–5; 26.15–16), thus implicitly accenting their paradisal character. But Teresa is not satisfied to make her point by general statements; she supports her testimony by a host of concrete examples of virtuous living by incorporating into her narrative the biographies of particular nuns in her foundations as well as of some friars. Far from being digressions, these *vitae* are integral to Teresa's story of how her foundations restored the earthly paradise that leads to heaven, the goal of the heroic quest of Teresa and her nuns. For example, Beatriz de la Encarnación, one of the first nuns of the Valladolid Carmel, possessed perfectly the virtues Teresa most esteemed: perpetual prayer, flawless obedience, the greatest charity toward neighbor, great humility, detachment from consolation, and patience in tremendous suffering. At the hour of Beatriz's death, all present are given a foretaste of what awaits those who have served the Lord in the earthly paradise of Teresa's monasteries:

A little before nine while all were with her (and [her confessor] too), about a quarter of an hour before she died, she raised her eyes, and a happiness like a shining light came over her countenance. She remained as would someone gazing on an object that gives profound joy, for she smiled twice. All those who were there, and the priest himself, received so much spiritual delight and happiness that they didn't know what else to say than it seemed to them they were in heaven. And with this happiness that I mention, her eyes fixed on heaven, she died, looking like an angel (12.8).

After her death, Beatriz's body had "an extremely sweet fragrance" (12.9), the so-called odor of sanctity. Similar occurrences are reported in Teresa's account of the death of a nun (Petronila de San Andrés) at St. Joseph's monastery in Toledo:

It happened that while I was here a fatal illness struck one of the Sisters. After receiving the sacraments and being anointed, her happiness and joy were so great that, as though she were going to another country, we were able to talk to her about how she should recommend us to God when in heaven and to the saints to whom we were devoted. A little before she died, I went to her room to be with her, for I had just gone before the Blessed Sacrament to beg the Lord to give her a good death. And when I entered I saw His Majesty at the head of the bed. His arms were partly opened as though He were protecting her. . . . After a little while I began to speak to her, and she said to me: "O Mother, what great things I am going to see." Thus she died, like an angel (16.4).

The interpolated profiles of Doña Casilda de Padilla (10.8–16; 11), Beatriz de la Madre de Dios (26.2–15), Jerónimo Gracián de la Madre de Dios (23), and Ambrosio Mariano (17.7–15), indicate that these already virtuous souls found in Carmel a safe path, removed from the dangers of the world, to heaven. In the same vein, the prayerful, mortified, and long-suffering Catalina Sandoval y Godínez, whose conversion and vocation led to the foundation of St. Joseph of the Savior monastery in Beas (22.4–24), had a dream about entering Carmel almost twenty years before she actually did so that left her with "a happiness that made her think she had been in heaven" (22.21).[19] Finally, the stories of the obedient servants of God—Teresa de Layz, who brought Teresa's nuns to Alba de Tormes (20.2–14) and Doña Catalina de Cardona, who brought the friars to a cave she inhabited near Villanueva de la Jara (28.21–36)—reveal that those who were instrumental in establishing foundations of the reformed Carmel, although not Carmelites themselves, shared in the favors God bestowed upon the Order. A married woman, Teresa de Layz was told in a vision of St. Andrew—the patron of childless couples—in a beautiful "green meadow with white flowers" (20.7) that she would find salvation not by bearing and raising children but by founding a monastery. The odor of sanctity emanated from Catalina de Cardona while she was still alive, and after her death this holy woman appeared "in a glorified body and some angels with her" (28.36) to Teresa just after she had received Communion in the church the friars had built at the place where Catalina's cave was located.

Fourth, St. Joseph's in Ávila as well as Teresa's subsequent foundations were images of the primitive Carmel. In chapter 2 of the *Foundations*, Teresa explains how, because St. Joseph's was a portrait of Carmel in its origins, she received permission from Father General to make further foundations. "He rejoiced to see our manner of life, a portrait, although an imperfect one, of the beginnings of our order, and how the primitive rule was being kept in all its rigor, for it wasn't being observed in any monastery in the entire order; only the mitigated rule was observed. And with the desire he had that this beginning go forward, he gave me very extensive patent letters, so that more monasteries could be founded" (2.3). The idea that St. Joseph's, and hence Teresa's subsequent foundations, were portraits of the primitive Carmel accentuates their paradisal character. The word *Carmel* means "garden" or "orchard." Because of its luxuriant verdure, Mt. Carmel was renowned in the biblical world for its fertility and beauty.[20] It was on Mt. Carmel where the Order of Our Lady of Mt. Carmel was founded circa 1200 when, it is conjectured, some Western inhabitants of the Latin kingdom of Jerusalem, probably pilgrims or crusaders, began to lead the eremitical life in imitation of the Old Testament prophet Elijah.[21] Teresa's reform of the Carmelites sought to return to the primitive spirit and observance of the order that flourished on Mt. Carmel. By her establishment of this spirit and observance at St. Joseph's in Ávila and her other foundations, Teresa then makes Mt. Carmel metaphorically bud, blossom, flower, and flourish again. The appropriateness of this metaphor is seen in the following passage, which reports Teresa's impression when the friars, whose reform she also inspired, came to meet their prior and Teresa and her nuns at Villanueva de la Jara. "Since they were discalced and wore their poor, coarse woolen mantles, they inspired us all with devotion and moved me to tender feelings since it seemed to me that I was present in that flourishing time of our holy Fathers of old. In that field, they appeared to be like white fragrant flowers, and indeed I believe that before God they are, for in my opinion He is authentically served there" (28.20). Likewise, in the dedicatory letter to his edition of Teresa's works, Luis de León describes Teresa and her nuns as "fair flowers which beautify the barrenness of these present times, the choicest branches of the Church."[22]

The Heroic Defense of the Earthly Paradise:

"[The] devil was displeased that so many houses were being founded where our Lord was being served" (27.20).

Teresa had to resist and overcome great civil and ecclesiastical opposition, instigated by the devil, in founding St. Joseph's in Ávila. Once founded, St. Joseph's had to be defended against the devil, who sought to enter it in order to change the earthly paradise into hell on earth. This same pattern recurs with each of Teresa's foundations after St. Joseph's, as her chronicle of these foundations and counsels to prioresses affirm.

St. Joseph's was founded by Teresa to express her gratitude to God for his benevolence on her behalf and her "great impulses to help souls" (*Life*, 32.6) lost by the Reformation. The latter purpose was achieved by means of Teresa's and her nuns' apostolate of prayer. At the beginning of the *Foundations,* Teresa's concern for souls is again center stage. A Franciscan missionary, recently returned from the New World, visited St. Joseph's and told Teresa and her sisters "about the many millions of souls that were being lost there for want of Christian instruction, and before leaving he gave us a sermon, or conference, encouraging us to do penance" (1.7). Teresa was extremely upset by this news:

> I was so grief-stricken over the loss of so many souls that I couldn't contain myself. I went to a hermitage with many tears. I cried out to the Lord, begging Him that He give me the means to be able to do something to win some souls to His service, since the devil was carrying away so many, and that my prayer would do some good since I wasn't able to do anything else. I was very envious of those who for love of our Lord were able to be engaged in winning souls, though they might suffer a thousand deaths. And thus it happens to me that when we read in the lives of the saints that they converted souls, I feel much greater devotion, tenderness, and envy than over all the martyrdoms they suffered. This is the inclination the Lord has given me, for it seems to me that He prizes a soul that through our diligence and prayer we gain for Him, through His mercy, more than all the services we can render Him (1.7).

For his part, the Lord responds by comforting Teresa with his presence and a promise. "Well, going about with such great affliction, while I was in prayer one night, our Lord represented Himself to me in His usual way. He showed me much love, manifesting His desire to comfort me, and said: 'Wait a little, daughter, and you will see great things' " (1.8).

Reading on in the *Foundations*, it becomes clear that the "great things" that the Lord promises are the monasteries he would work to establish through his friend, Teresa. In these monasteries the Lord would be well served, and souls would be gained for him through the "diligence and prayer" (1.7) of Teresa and her nuns. God's friends "do not simply claim God for themselves; they also share in the rule and responsibility of God for the world."[23] Teresa's foundations and the life-style and apostolate of prayer for the salvation of souls observed therein manifest this dimension of the friendship of the saint and her nuns with God. Moreover, each of Teresa's foundations, where the Blessed Sacrament was reserved in the chapel or adjacent church, replaced those churches destroyed by the Protestants. "This is a special consolation for me to see one more church, particularly when I recall the many that the Lutherans are suppressing" (18.5; cf. 3.10). As a result, Teresa and her nuns again find themselves in the heat of the battle raging between, on the one hand, God and his Church and, on the other, Satan and his minions.

Teresa is fully conscious of the devil's opposition to her carrying out the Lord's work of establishing monasteries of the reformed Carmel as the following passages confirm:

> When You, Lord, want to give courage, how little do all contradictions matter! Rather, it seems I am encouraged by them, thinking that since the devil is beginning to be disturbed the Lord will be served in that monastery (3.4).

I already have experience of what the devil stirs up to hinder one of these monasteries. . . . I believe that God is served very much in it since the devil cannot bear it (18.2).

[The] devil was displeased that so many houses were being founded where our Lord was being served (27.20).

It was clearly seen how much the devil resented this holy beginning, which our Lord had initiated, and also that this was the Lord's own work since it was growing (28.1).

In the case of her Burgos foundation, Teresa heard these ominous words from the Lord: "'The devil uses all his strength to hinder that foundation; use yours with my help so that it may be realized and do not fail to go in person, for great good will be done'" (31.11). The devil always stirred up civil and ecclesiastical opposition to Teresa's foundations. He would also attempt to frustrate God's work by afflicting Teresa with depression, vacillation, indecision, and repugnance toward going ahead with her foundations. In some places the devil opposed Teresa more fiercely than others. For instance, Teresa says that the foundation of St. Joseph's in Seville, where "the devils have greater leeway . . . to tempt souls" (25.1), was the costliest foundation after St. Joseph's in Ávila. "In my opinion, aside from the first foundation in Ávila (for with that one there is no comparison), none of the other foundations cost me as much as this one did in which the trials were for the most part interior ones" (26.2). Similarly, in Palencia the devil caused "blindness in many matters" (29.23), because at the site the Lord chose for

Teresa's monastery "many things could be done that the devil was sad to see taken away" (29.23).

In St. Gregory the Great's commentary on the Book of Job that Teresa read during one of her illnesses while she was at the monastery of the Incarnation (see *Life*, 5.8), the idea is found that the devil can act anywhere in the world at anytime but always and only with God's permission.[24] Therefore, the devil's assaults against Teresa in her efforts to establish her foundations occur with the Lord's permission. "[The] Lord desired that no foundation be made without some trial in one way or another" (24.15; cf. 15.8). In Gregory's thought, the devil "made 'war' on man in paradise, trying his loyalty to God," but this temptation "was also God's test of man's obedience."[25] According to Teresa, God allows the trials she and her nuns experienced to test them in suffering (see 28.3). While humanity failed its test of loyalty to God in Eden, Teresa and her sisters are successful in overcoming the trials they suffer in their efforts to fulfill God's plan of restoring the earthly paradise. Furthermore, suffering affords them the opportunity to imitate the heroic Passion of Christ (see 28.43; *Secular Scripture*, 88). Thus, Teresa and her nuns are doubly heroic.

The devil often took revenge on Teresa and her sisters for his defeat. For example, when a fire broke out at the solemn reservation of the Blessed Sacrament at the Seville Carmel, Teresa commented, "The devil must have been so angry at seeing another house of God and the solemnity that was demonstrated that he wanted somehow to get revenge. But His Majesty did not allow this; may He be blessed forever, amen" (25.14). On no account, however, did the devil surrender. On the contrary, once the devil failed to prevent the restoration of the earthly paradise by Teresa's foundations, he sought to enter and destroy her monasteries from within. What accounted for the transformation of the unenclosed monastery of the Incarnation from purgatory on earth to "a step on the way toward hell" (*Life,* 7.3) was its openness, which made it possible for the world and evil influences to enter. Accordingly in the *Foundations* Teresa exhorts her sisters, "[Beware], for the devil through very small things drills holes through which very large things enter" (29.32). To this end, Teresa sternly admonishes her sisters against any mitigation of the primitive rule, especially with regard to enclosure:

> May it please His Majesty to give us abundant grace, for with this, nothing will prevent us from advancing ever in His service. And may He protect and favor all of us so that this excellent beginning, which He was pleased to initiate in women as miserable as we, may not be lost through our weakness. In His name I beg you, my daughters and Sisters, that you always ask our Lord for this and that each one who enters in the future bear in mind that with her the observance of the primitive rule of the order of the Virgin, our Lady, begins again and that she must in no way consent to any mitigation. Consider that through very little things the door is opened to very big things, and that without your realizing it the world will start entering your lives. Remember the poverty and hardship that was undergone in obtaining what you now quietly enjoy. If you note carefully, you will see that in part these houses, most of them, have not been founded by men but by the powerful hand of God and that His Majesty is very fond of

advancing the works He accomplishes provided
we cooperate (27.11; cf. 29.33; 31.46).

Moreover, in chapters 4–8 of the *Foundations*, Teresa speaks
to prioresses about specific areas of conventual life that
they must carefully monitor, lest the devil use them to
wreak havoc in the monastery.

One such area is obedience. "[Since] the devil sees
there is no path that leads more quickly to the highest
perfection than obedience, he sets up many annoyances
and difficulties under the color of good" (5.10). Related to
obedience is the question of how to deal with melancholic
persons, for melancholy is the devil's "means for trying to
win over some persons" (7.2). "If we consider the matter,
that which interests these melancholic persons most is
getting their own way, saying everything that comes to
their lips, looking at the faults of others with which they
hide their own, and finding rest in what gives them
pleasure; in sum, they are like a person who cannot bear
anyone who resists them. Well, if the passions go
unmortified, and each passion seeks to get what it wants,
what would happen if no one resisted them?" (7.3). Teresa
regards melancholy as "a sickness more prejudicial to all
perfection than that of those who are in bed and in
danger of death" (7.10), and, if left unchecked, it can
become "a death capable of killing all the nuns" (7.10).
The only remedy for this "terrible artifice of the devil"
(7.3) is submission in obedience to the prioress in all
things. While this may make the life of persons suffering
from this affliction purgatory on earth, it assures them of
heaven in the hereafter (see 7.5).

Another cause for concern in community life is delusions concerning rapture, because they bind the person so
afflicted "as to hinder growth. The soul here resembles

someone on a journey who enters a quagmire or swamp and thus cannot move onward. And, in order to advance, a soul must not only walk but fly" (6.15). Appropriately, Teresa depicts the effect of these delusions by imagery that connotes that the soul in this state is held captive in the demonic world and thus cannot ascend to God who is in higher worlds. In a similar vein, revelations and visions, Teresa advises, must be approached with caution, because sometimes "the devil so as to incite pride causes these apparitions" (8.4). The ruse the devil uses to deceive the soul is to make it think that it deserves these favors because of some service it has done or its own holiness. Humility is the safeguard against this deception, "[for] if this path is from the spirit of the Lord, it brings with it the humility to like being despised" (8.9). For her part, "the prioress, with prudence, should always be seen as tending more to praise those who distinguish themselves in matters pertaining to humility, mortification, and obedience than those God leads by this very supernatural path of prayer, even though the latter may have all these other virtues" (8.9).

Even though Teresa and her nuns are in the earthly paradise of the monastery, they are subject, as Adam and Eve were in Eden, to temptations by the devil that test their loyalty and obedience to God. While Teresa had restored the earthly paradise by her foundations, she and her nuns must maintain and preserve it by resisting temptation, which also testifies to their heroism. However, God assures Teresa of his special protection of the nuns who die in her monasteries. "He told me that I could be certain He would protect all the nuns that die in these monasteries and that they should not fear temptation at the hour of death" (16.4). Indeed Teresa adds, "And I have noticed that some who have died since this occurred [that is, God's promise of protection] have done so with quiet and calm as though they were in rapture or in the prayer of quiet, without showing the least sign of any temptation" (16.5).

To summarize, although the archetypes of romance—the ascent to heaven, the restoration of the earthly paradise, and the heroic defense of the earthly paradise—are not as neatly sequentially ordered in the *Foundations* as they are in the *Life*, the *Way of Perfection*, and the *Interior Castle*, nonetheless, they are present, giving this work a clear thematic and narrative unity. In fact, the *Foundations* amplify and elaborate on these archetypes with a plethora of examples and material not found in Teresa's other three major prose works. In short, the *Foundations* possesses a richness that has not always been done justice by scholars.

Conclusion

In a recent effort to define the nature of spiritual theology, James A. Wiseman specifies that this theological discipline concentrates on "the human person's attempt to live by the Spirit according to the highest Christian ideals in response to God's self-giving."[1] In the history of Christian spirituality, St. Teresa stands out as both a model and guide for those striving to respond to God's self-donation in their lives. Teresa's writings, especially the *Life*, the *Way of Perfection*, the *Interior Castle*, and the *Foundations*, record her example and guidance, namely, her spiritual theology. The preceding pages have demonstrated that Teresa's spiritual theology, as presented in these four texts, is essentially narrative in form, an aspect of the saint's writings that has been neglected in the existent corpus of commentaries. More specifically, we have seen that Teresa's spiritual theology—be it her life story, articulation and dissemination of the Teresian Carmelite ideal, or teaching on prayer and the development of the interior life—is encoded in images that form archetypes that in turn make up a sequence or narrative.

These images and archetypes are neither incidental nor dispensable if the richness and integrity of Teresa's spiritual theology is to be recovered. For example, this study has brought to light a group of images in the saint's works that have been overlooked by Teresian scholars: hell, the earthly paradise, and heaven. These images, together with the world of ordinary experience, constitute the universe in which Teresa's life, mystical experience, Carmelite ideal and reform, and teaching on the spiritual life unfold. Moreover, Teresa's most well-known images—the garden, the way/path/road, the castle, the fountain, the silkworm/ butterfly, betrothal and marriage, light and darkness—are part of this universe by their very nature. This interrelationship, indeed interdependence, of Teresa's images within a single work as well as among her four major prose works underscores the fundamental coherence of these texts and consequently of her spiritual doctrine.

This study has given much attention to the images in which Teresa enfleshes her spiritual experience and teaching in her writings. However, I want to conclude by focusing on an image found in the interior of baroque churches that is the visual counterpart to some of Teresa's imagery. The hallmark of baroque church interiors is that the ceiling gives the impression of having been shattered or dissolved to reveal an upper celestial world of cloud and light. The impact on the spectator is profound: "[The] individual participates in a spectacle which . . . translates him bodily upward as he gazes into a supernatural and infinite world."[2] To explain this "break-through" of heaven to earth, the art historian Frederick Hartt has turned to the writings of the Counter-Reformation mystics, particularly St. Teresa:

In the ordinary day-to-day assumptions of seventeenth century religious imagery the force which brings about such a break-through is the redemptive power of divine love. The great mystics of the Counter-Reformation devoted their writings chiefly to the union of the soul with God by means of a sudden obliteration of all intervening barriers. This union is described as a union of love, and is frequently accompanied by the most passionate imagery. No longer are theologians occupied with the construction of a universal hierarchy of knowledge, but only with the tracing of a path through darkness up to God, leaving all temporal and spiritual goods, even reason, far below. St. Teresa, St. John of the Cross, St. Philip of the Holy Trinity, St. Philip Neri, St. Mary Magdalen dei Pazzi, despite individual differences of temperament, are concerned wholly with the union of the soul with God through love, a union which can take place in this life and is a prefiguration of the joys of the next.[3]

Although in this passage he names several mystics whose writings treat the union of the soul with God, Hartt continues by documenting his insight with quotations principally from Teresa.[4]

Like the baroque church ceiling that they may have helped inspire,[5] Teresa's writings direct our gaze upward but also inward. Surpassing all others, the images of heaven and the earthly paradise, itself a figure of the celestial paradise, prevail in Teresa's works.[6] Why is there a preponderance of the divine, the supernatural, and the heavenly world in Teresa's life and doctrine? It is due to God's tremendous love for Teresa and in turn Teresa's passionate love of God.[7] Again, we are brought back to romance, for the "central element of romance is a love story" (*Secular Scripture,* 24). Teresa's writings are the divine romance *par excellence.*

Notes

Introduction

1 For a view of the city of Ávila in 1570, see Richard L. Kagan, ed., *Spanish Cities of the Golden Age: The Views of Anton van den Wyngaerde* (Berkeley, Calif.: University of California Press, 1989), 356–58. The principal source of information about Teresa's life is, of course, her own autobiography and other writings. In preparing the biographical sketch of Teresa that follows, I have also drawn upon the following secondary sources, which will not be further documented unless quoted: Jodi Bilinkoff, *The Ávila of St. Teresa: Religious Reform in a Sixteenth-Century City* (Ithaca, N.Y.: Cornell University Press, 1989); Joseph F. Chorpenning, "Reading St. Teresa of Ávila's *Life* Today," *Spirituality Today* 36 (1984): 196–219; Stephen Clissold, *St. Teresa of Ávila* (London: Sheldon Press, 1979); Margaret Dorgan, "St. Teresa of Ávila: Woman and Waverer," *Cross Currents* 32 (1982): 155–59; Teófanes Egido, "The Historical Setting of St. Teresa's Life," *Carmelite Studies* 1 (1980): 122–82; Kieran Kavanaugh's introductions and notes to his and Otilio Rodríguez's translation of *The Collected Works of St. Teresa of Ávila*, 3 vols. (Washington, D.C.: Institute of Carmelite Studies Publications, 1976–82) and his "St. Teresa and the Spirituality of Sixteenth-Century Spain," in *The Roots of the Modern Christian Tradition*, ed. E. Rozanne Elder (Kalamazoo, Mich.: Cistercian Publications, 1984), 91–104; and Ciriaco Morón Arroyo, "The Human Value of the Divine: St. Teresa of Jesus" in *Women Writers of the Renaissance and Reformation*, ed. Katharina M. Wilson (Athens, Ga.: University of Georgia Press, 1987), 401–431.

2   Egido, 140.

3   Clissold, 3.

4   Joseph N. Tylenda, intro., trans., and commentary, *A Pilgrim's Journey: The Autobiography of Ignatius of Loyola* (Wilmington, Del.: Michael Glazier, 1985), 11–12. For an introduction to the Spanish chivalric romances, see Daniel Eisenberg, *Romances of Chivalry in the Spanish Golden Age* (Newark, Del.: Juan de la Cuesta Hispanic Monographs, 1982).

5   Quoted by Kavanaugh, "Introduction" to the *Life,* in *Collected Works of St. Teresa of Ávila,* I: 2.

6   See *A Pilgrim's Journey,* 11–13.

7   Bilinkoff, 115.

8   The classic study of the influence of Erasmus on sixteenth-century Spanish spirituality is Marcel Bataillon's *Erasmo y España: Estudios sobre la historia espiritual del siglo XVI,* trans. Antonio Alatorre, 2nd ed. (Mexico City: Fondo de Cultura Económica, 1966). On the presence of Protestant literature in sixteenth-century Spain, see A. Gordon Kinder, "Printing and Reformation Ideas in Spain," *Bulletin of the Society for Spanish and Portuguese Historical Studies* 14 (1989): 10–24.

9   On the history and development of the Inquisition, see Henry Kamen, *Inquisition and Society in Spain in the Sixteenth and Seventeenth Centuries* (Bloomington, Ind.: Indiana University Press, 1985); on Teresa and the Inquisition, see Enrique Llamas Martínez's important book *Santa Teresa de Jesús y la Inquisición española* (Madrid: Consejo Superior de Investigaciones Científicas, 1972).

10 H. Outram Evennett, *The Spirit of the Counter-Reformation,* ed. John Bossy (Notre Dame, Ind.: University of Notre Dame Press, 1975), 78.

11 *A Pilgrim's Journey,* 59.

12 Evennett, 79.

13 Elias L. Rivers, "The Vernacular Mind of St. Teresa," *Carmelite Studies* 3 (1984): 113–29, especially 120–25.

14 Elias L. Rivers, *Quixotic Scriptures: Essays on the Textuality of Hispanic Literature* (Bloomington, Ind.: Indiana University Press, 1983), 68.

15   See Erich Auerbach, *"Sermo Humilis,"* in *Literary Language and Its Public in Late Latin Antiquity and in the Middle Ages,* trans. Ralph Manheim (New York: Pantheon Books, 1965), 27–66.

16   Rivers, "Vernacular Mind of St. Teresa," 121.

17   Ibid., 123–24.

18   Bilinkoff, 111.

19   See Víctor García de la Concha, *El arte literario de Santa Teresa* (Barcelona: Editorial Ariel, 1978), 47–90.

20   See Ruth P. Liebowitz, "Virgins in the Service of Christ: The Dispute over an Active Apostolate for Women during the Counter-Reformation," in *Women of Spirit: Female Leadership in the Jewish and Christian Traditions,* eds. Rosemary Ruether and Eleanor McLaughlin (New York: Simon and Schuster, 1979), 132–52.

21   Bilinkoff, 150.

22   Roy Pascal, *Design and Truth in Autobiography* (Cambridge, Mass.: Harvard University Press, 1960), 9 and 11, respectively.

23   Ibid., 31.

24   See Karl J. Weintraub, *The Value of the Individual: Self and Circumstance in Autobiography* (Chicago: University of Chicago Press, 1978), 218; Pascal, 26–27.

25   *Collected Works of St. Teresa of Ávila,* II: 445.

26   Morón Arroyo, 404.

27   Joseph A. Nelson, ed., *Roman Breviary in English: Autumn* (New York: Benziger Brothers, 1950), 591–92. Cf. Elvira Sarmiento and a Carmelite of Grand Rapids, Mich., trans., *Depositions of the Processes of St. Teresa of Jesus* (Carmel of Flemington, N.J., 1969), *passim.*

28   Kavanaugh, "Introduction" to the *Meditations on the Song of Songs* in *Collected Works of St. Teresa of Ávila,* II: 209–10.

29   *Collected Works of St. Teresa of Ávila,* I: 172–73.

30   See *A Pilgrim's Journey,* 35–39.

31   E. Allison Peers, trans., in *The Complete Works of St. Teresa of Jesus*, 3
vols. (1946; London: Sheed and Ward, 1978), 3: 369–70.

32   "Apostolic Letter of Our Most Holy Lord Paul VI by Divine Provi-
dence Pope when Saint Teresa of Ávila Is Declared Doctor of the
Church," trans., Carmelite nuns of Louisville, Ky., in *Contemplative
Prayer according to the Writings of St. Teresa of Jesus and St. John of
the Cross, Doctors of the Church*, ed. José L. Morales (Brooklyn
Carmel, n.d.), i–ix, at iv. I am grateful to Father John Sullivan,
O.C.D., for providing me with a copy of this English translation of
Paul VI's letter.

33   In *Complete Works of St. Teresa of Jesus* 3: 368–69.

34   Irving Lavin, *Bernini and the Unity of the Visual Arts*, 2 vols. (New
York: Pierpont Morgan Library and Oxford University Press, 1980) 1:
132. See also Laura Gutiérrez Rueda, "Santa Teresa, escritora," in
Ensayo de iconografía teresiana, número monográfico de *Revista de
espiritualidad* 23 (1964): 61–78.

35   E. Allison Peers, trans., *The Letters of St. Teresa of Jesus*, 2 vols. (1951;
London: Sheed and Ward, 1980) 1: 412.

36   See Rivers, "Vernacular Mind of St. Teresa," 123–27.

37   Kavanaugh, "Introduction" to the *Life*, in *Collected Works of St. Teresa
of Ávila*, I: 28.

38   The evaluation of Teresa's individual works is fully documented at
the beginning of each chapter of this book.

39   See García de la Concha, *passim*; Mary C. Sullivan, "From Narrative
to Proclamation: A Rhetorical Analysis of the Autobiography of
Teresa of Ávila," *Thought* 58 (1983): 453–71; Carole Slade, "St. Teresa's
Meditaciones sobre los Cantares: The Hermeneutics of Humility and
Enjoyment," *Religion & Literature* 18 (1986): 27–44; Alison Weber,
Teresa of Ávila and the Rhetoric of Femininity (Princeton, N.J.: Princeton
University Press, 1990); and Elizabeth B. Davis, "De nuevo, sobre la
'literariedad' de Teresa de Jesús," *Anuario de Letras* (Mexico) 28
(1990): 159–80.

40   See Salvador Ros García, "Los estudios teresianos: Panorama de
actualidad y perspectivas de tratamiento," *Teresianum* 38 (1987):
149–209. Theologians have not been unaware of the importance
of Teresa's works for narrative theology. For example, Harvey D.
Egan has noted that "the concreteness of [Teresa's] writings establishes

a point of contact with the contemporary interest in narrative theology, a theology that refuses to detach itself from the great Christian stories, images, poetry, and myths" (*Christian Mysticism: The Future of a Tradition* [New York: Pueblo Publishing Co., 1984], 163). A rudimentary effort to relate Teresa's *Life* to narrative theology may be found in Chorpenning, 202–209. Jürgen Moltmann has observed that "Teresa's theology is her biography, and her biography is her theology" ("Teresa of Ávila and Martin Luther: The Turn to the Mysticism of the Cross," *Studies in Religion* 13 [1984]: 265–78, especially 269).

41 *Collected Works of St. Teresa of Ávila*, I: 35.

42 See Charles F. Altman, "Two Types of Opposition and the Structure of Latin Saints' Lives," *Medievalia et Humanistica* 6 (1975): 1–11; and Alison Goddard Elliot, *Roads to Paradise: Reading the Lives of the Early Saints* (Hanover, N.H.: University Press of New England, 1987).

43 See Joseph F. Chorpenning, "St. Teresa's Presentation of Her Religious Experience," *Carmelite Studies* 3 (1984): 152–88, especially 167–70.

44 See Dámaso Alonso, *La poesía de San Juan de la Cruz: Desde esta ladera*, 4th ed. (Madrid: Aguilar, 1966), 37–77; and Javier Herrero, "The Knight and the Mystical Castle," *Studies in Formative Spirituality* 4 (1983): 393–407, especially 402–403.

45 Herrero, 395–96.

46 Herrero, 400.

47 Herrero, 399; *A Pilgrim's Journey*, 25–27.

48 *A Pilgrim's Journey*, 31.

49 Herrero, 404–405.

50 Herrero, 405–407.

51 See Stephen Crites, "The Narrative Quality of Experience," *Journal of the American Academy of Religion* 39 (1971): 291–311.

52 See George W. Stroup, "A Bibliographical Critique," *Theology Today* 32 (1975): 133–43, especially 140.

53 Stroup specifically mentions Frye's literary criticism as being particularly helpful to narrative theologians, because it provides "formal criteria for a more exact determination of the nature of narrative" (140). The importance of Frye's theories for historiography has also recently been recognized. See Hayden White, *Metahistory: The Historical Imagination in Nineteenth-Century Europe* (Baltimore: Johns Hopkins University Press, 1973) and "The Historical Text as Literary Artifact," in *Tropics of Discourse: Essays in Cultural Criticism* (Baltimore: Johns Hopkins University Press, 1985), 81–100. Although Frye makes no mention of Teresa in his works, he does refer to St. John of the Cross in his latest and last book *Words with Power*. Frye cites John's influence on T. S. Eliot (160–61, 290) and describes John's imagery as mainly that of ascent (161, 206).

Chapter 1 The *Life*

1 E. Allison Peers, *Mother of Carmel: A Portrait of St. Teresa of Jesus* (1944; Wilton, Conn.: Morehouse-Barlow, 1979), 51; and Helmut A. Hatzfeld, "Santa Teresa de Jesus (1515–1582): El huerto del alma," *Explicación de textos literarios* 1, anejo 1 (1973): 39–45, especially 40. See also Mary C. Sullivan, "From Narrative to Proclamation: A Rhetorical Analysis of the Autobiography of Teresa of Ávila," *Thought* 58 (1983): 453–71, especially 459–60.

2 Víctor García de la Concha, *El arte literario de Santa Teresa* (Barcelona: Editorial Ariel, 1978), 184–227; Guido Mancini, "Estudio preliminar" to his edition of Santa Teresa de Jesús, *Libro de la vida* (Madrid: Taurus, 1982), 27–28; and Ricardo Senabre, "Sobre el género literario del *Libro de la vida*," in *Actas del Congreso Internacional Teresiano, Salamanca, 4–7 Octubre 1982*, eds. Teófanes Egido et al., 2 vols. (Salamanca: Universidad de Salamanca, 1983) 2: 765–76, especially 773–76.

3 See Senabre, 769–70. According to one of Teresa's biographers, the saint and her brother Rodrigo even wrote a romance of chivalry. See Francisco de Ribera, *Vida de Santa Teresa de Jesús*, ed. J. Pons (1590; Barcelona: Gustavo Gili, 1908), 99. For a summary of the scholarship on Teresa's reading of the chivalric romances, see Francisco Márquez Villanueva, "La vocación literaria de Santa Teresa," *Nueva Revista de Filología Hispánica* 32 (1983): 355–79, especially 356, note 4. Javier Herrero has recently discussed the formative influence of these romances on the metaphors Teresa uses to express her religious experience. See "The Knight and the Mystical Castle," *Studies in Formative Spirituality* 4 (1983): 393–407.

4   It was a commonplace in medieval and Renaissance art and litera-
     ture that the opening through which hell was entered was its
     mouth. See Gary D. Smith, *The Mouth of Hell in Medieval Art and
     Thought*, diss. University of Illinois at Urbana-Champaign, 1985
     (Ann Arbor, Mich.: University Microfilms, 1987); cf. *Words with
     Power*, 260. Interestingly, an illustration of the mouth of hell appears
     in an anonymous early seventeenth-century book of emblems, en-
     titled *Idea vitae teresianae iconibus symbolicis expressa . . .*, depicting
     Teresa's spiritual doctrine. See Santiago Sebastián López, "Iconografía
     de la vida mística teresiana," *Boletín del Museo e Instituto "Camón
     Aznar"* 10 (1982): 15–68, especially 61 (figure 74).

5   This overview is based on St. Athanasius, *The Life of St. Antony*, trans.
     Robert T. Meyer, Ancient Christian Writers, no. 10 (Westminster,
     Md.: Newman Press, 1950); Boniface Ramsey, *Beginning to Read the
     Fathers* (New York: Paulist Press, 1985), 149–63; Joachim Smet, *The
     Carmelites: A History of the Brothers of Our Lady of Mt. Carmel*, 4 vols.
     (Darien, Ill.: Carmelite Spiritual Center, 1975–85) 1:1–23, 85–87;
     Bede Edwards, trans., *The Rule of St. Albert* (Aylesford: Carmelite
     Priory, 1973); and David Knowles, *The Religious Orders in England*, 3
     vols. (1948–59; Cambridge: Cambridge University Press, 1979) 1:
     195–99.

6   *Life of St. Antony*, 33.

7   Ibid., 22.

8   See Margaret Dorgan, "St. Teresa of Ávila: Woman and Waverer,"
     Cross Currents 32 (1982): 155–59, especially 156; and Jodi Bilinkoff,
     "The Social Meaning of Religious Reform: The Case of St. Teresa and
     Ávila," *Archiv für Reformationsgeschichte* 79 (1988): 340–57, especially
     346–47.

9   See Herbert Friedmann, *A Bestiary for St. Jerome: Animal Symbolism in
     European Religious Art* (Washington, D.C.: Smithsonian Institution
     Press, 1980), 218.

10   On Teresa's devotion to the Passion in the context of the religious
     culture of her day, see Jan Rhodes, "St. Teresa and Devotion to
     Christ's Passion: 'I am only asking you to look at Him,'" *Mount
     Carmel* 27 (1979): 108–37.

11   Catherine Romano, "A Psycho-Spiritual History of Teresa of Ávila: A
     Woman's Perspective," in *Western Spirituality: Historical Roots, Ecu-
     menical Routes*, ed. Matthew Fox (Notre Dame, Ind.: Fides/Claretian
     Press, 1979), 261–95, especially 286.

12 See Elizabeth B. Davis, "De nuevo, sobre la 'literariedad' de Teresa de Jesús," *Anuario de Letras* (Mexico) 28 (1990): 159–80, especially 162–63, 166.

13 García de la Concha remarks in passing that the garden of chapters 11–22 of the *Life* reflects the biblical garden of the Song of Songs 2.16, 4.12, and 6.2ff (245–46). See also Stanley Stewart, *The Enclosed Garden: The Tradition and Image in Seventeenth-Century Poetry* (Madison, Wis.: University of Wisconsin Press, 1966), 109, 124.

14 See *Life of St. Antony*, 22–31; Ramsey 150, 156–57.

15 For a discussion of and bibliography on the demonology of the *Life*, see Enrique Llamas, "*Libro de la vida*" in *Introducción a la lectura de Santa Teresa*, ed. Alberto Barrientos (Madrid: Editorial de Espiritualidad, 1978), 205–39, especially 231–36 and "Santa Teresa de Jesús y la religiosidad popular," *Revista de Espiritualidad* 40 (1981): 215–52, especially 237–51.

16 For a detailed analysis of chapter 32 of the *Life*, see Rosendo Roig, "De la visión del infierno a la visión del primer Carmelo: Comentario estilístico del capítulo XXXII del *Libro de la vida* de Santa Teresa," *Letras de Deusto* 12 (1982): 59–75.

17 See Llamas, "*Libro de la vida*," 233 and "Santa Teresa de Jesús y la religiosidad popular," 242. For a fine analysis of the civil and ecclesiastical opposition to Teresa's reform, see Bilinkoff's article cited in note 8.

18 The source of the image of the *hortus conclusus* is Song of Songs 4.12.

19 The expression *paradise of delights* reflects the Vulgate reading of Genesis 2.8, which other versions normally have rendered otherwise: "Plantaverat autem Dominus Deus paradisum voluptatis a principio, in quo posuit hominem quem formaverat."

20 Jean Leclercq, *The Life of Perfection: Points of View on the Essence of the Religious State*, trans. Leonard J. Doyle (Collegeville, Minn.: Liturgical Press, 1961), 119–25. See also Ramsey, 152–53.

21 The relationship between the imagery of chapters 11–22 and chapter 35 of the *Life* has been commented on by Joseph F. Chorpenning, "The Monastery, Paradise, and the Castle: Literary Images and Spiritual Development in St. Teresa of Ávila," *Bulletin of Hispanic Studies* 62 (1985): 245–57, especially 251–52.

22 Kieran Kavanaugh, "Introduction" to the *Way of Perfection* in *Collected Works of St. Teresa of Ávila*, II: 19.

23 See Herrero, 402–3.

Chapter 2 The *Way of Perfection*

1 See E. Allison Peers, *Mother of Carmel: A Portrait of St. Teresa of Jesus* (1944; Wilton, Conn.: Morehouse-Barlow, 1979), 70–71; Daniel de Pablo Maroto, "*Camino de perfección*," in *Introducción a la lectura de Santa Teresa*, ed. Alberto Barrientos (Madrid: Editorial de Espiritualidad, 1978), 269–310, especially 277–78; and Guido Mancini, *Teresa de Ávila: La libertà del sublime* (Pisa: Giardini Editori, 1981), 145.

2 Peers, 65–66.

3 Kieran Kavanaugh, "Introduction" to the *Way of Perfection* in *Collected Works of St. Teresa of Ávila*, II: 16.

4 The idea of monastic life as spiritual warfare (*militia spiritualis*) is integral to the Carmelite tradition as the following passage, inspired by various scriptural texts, from the primitive Carmelite *Rule of St. Albert* evidences: "Since man's life on earth is a time of trial . . . and the devil your foe is on the prowl like a roaring lion looking for prey to devour, you must use every care to clothe yourselves in God's armour so that you may be ready to withstand the enemy's ambush" (*The Rule of St. Albert*, Bede Edwards, trans. [Aylesford: Carmelite Priory, 1973] 87). For an overview of the biblical and Patristic background of this idea, see Adolar Zumkeller, *Augustine's Ideal of the Religious Life*, trans. Edmund Colledge (New York: Fordham University Press, 1986), 116–18.

5 Kavanaugh instructively comments on these remarks of Teresa. "What had occurred is that some harsh rumors had reached Teresa, but her remarks show that her knowledge of the facts was vague. It must be remembered that her references to the Lutherans in France represent her hazy way of speaking of Protestantism and demonstrate neither historical nor geographical precision. The unhappy news that had spread even to the enclosure of St. Joseph's concerned the religious war between the Catholics and Huguenots. Teresa's stereotypical remarks reflect the way the ordinary people in Spain probably commented on the news" ("Introduction" to the *Way* in *Collected Works of St. Teresa of Ávila*, II: 20). The Lutheran theologian

Jürgen Moltmann's observation on Teresa's remarks is also of interest. "Apart from the fact that we are dealing with Calvinist Christians in France at that time and not with Lutheran Christians, the spirit of the times is unmistakably present in Teresa's comments: the apocalyptic excitement which had seized not only the Reformers but also the Counter-Reformers and the absolutist struggle for the 'one true saving faith,' on the one hand, and the struggle for the 'one true saving Church' on the other" ("Teresa of Ávila and Martin Luther: The Turn to the Mysticism of the Cross," *Studies in Religion* 13 [1984]: 265–78, especially 266).

6   Moltmann, 265.

7   The association of St. Joseph's monastery with a castle or fortress was very appropriate, for the conjunction of monasteries and fortresses or royal palaces was a distinctive feature of the Iberian peninsula during the Middle Ages and the Renaissance. The classic example of this conjunction was the Escorial, the construction of which began in 1562. See Wolfgang Braunfels, *Monasteries of Western Europe: The Architecture of the Orders*, trans. Alastair Lang (Princeton, N.J.: Princeton University Press, 1980), 192, 196–200.

8   The *Rule of St. Albert* states: "Each one of you is to stay in his own cell or nearby, pondering the Lord's law day and night and keeping watch at his prayers unless attending to some other duty" (83).

9   The topic of friendship in Teresa's spirituality is an important and complex one that merits a monograph in itself. For an overview, based on Teresa's letters, of the manifold relationships she sustained, see Kevin Culligan, "Teresa of Jesus: A Personality Profile," *Spiritual Life* 29 (1983): 131–62, especially 146–57. See also Thomas Dubay's exposition of Teresa's teaching on friendship in his *Fire Within: St. Teresa of Ávila, St. John of the Cross, and the Gospel—on Prayer* (San Francisco: Ignatius Press, 1989), 271–88. Cf. Wendy M. Wright, *Bond of Perfection: Jeanne de Chantal & François de Sales* (New York: Paulist Press, 1985), 115.

10 Honor had multiple levels of meaning in sixteenth-century Spain: lineage (longevity of family lines); racial purity (freedom from the "stain" of Jewish or Moorish blood); life-style or behavior ("base" manual labor, including trade and commerce, was never to be engaged in; rather, income was to be drawn from landed estates); sexuality (women were expected to maintain virginity before marriage and fidelity to their husbands thereafter). See Jodi Bilinkoff, "The Social Meaning of Religious Reform: The Case of St. Teresa and Ávila," *Archiv für Reformationsgeschichte* 79 (1988): 340–57, especially

342–43. As is now well known, Teresa was of Jewish descent on her father's side. See Teófanes Egido, *El linaje judeoconverso de Santa Teresa: Pleito de hidalguía de los Cepeda* (Madrid: Editorial de Espiritualidad, 1986).

11 For an overview of this image in Teresa's writings, see Luis Maldonado, *Experiencia religiosa y lenguaje en Santa Teresa* (Madrid: Promoción Popular Cristiana, 1982), 15–62. See also Elizabeth T. Howe, *Mystical Imagery: Santa Teresa de Jesús and San Juan de la Cruz* (New York: Peter Lang, 1988), 242–50. Throughout the *Way*, Teresa uses the Spanish word *camino* for road/way/path. See Jeannine Poitrey, *Vocabulario de Santa Teresa* (Madrid: Fundación Universitaria Española, 1983), 125–26. Poitrey's references to the *Way* are to its first redaction, that is, the Escorial version.

12 Cf. Howe 249; and Thomas à Kempis, *The Imitation of Christ*, bk. 2, chap. 12, entitled "On the Royal Road of the Holy Cross" (see Leo Sherley-Price's translation [New York: Penguin Books, 1988] 84–89). The *Imitation* is believed to have been one of Teresa's favorite books. She recommended it to her nuns for spiritual reading. See Víctor García de la Concha, *El arte literario de Santa Teresa* (Barcelona: Editorial Ariel, 1978), 57.

13 The fountain is an element of the landscape of both the earthly paradise and heaven. See *Great Code*, 144–45 and Colleen McDannell and Bernhard Lang, *Heaven: A History* (New Haven, Conn.: Yale University Press, 1988), 119–22, 142–44.

14 This parallel has been studied by Joseph F. Chorpenning, "The Monastery, Paradise, and the Castle: Literary Images and Spiritual Development in St. Teresa of Ávila," *Bulletin of Hispanic Studies* 62 (1985): 245–57, especially 251–52.

15 Catherine Swietlicki, *Spanish Christian Cabala: The Works of Luis de León, Santa Teresa de Jesús, and San Juan de la Cruz* (Columbia, Mo.: University of Missouri Press, 1986), 57.

Chapter 3 The *Interior Castle*

1 E. Allison Peers, "Introduction" to his translation of the *Interior Castle* (Garden City, N.Y.: Image Books, 1961), 10.

2 Helmut A. Hatzfeld, *Santa Teresa de Ávila* (New York: Twayne Publishers, 1969), 42 and 59, respectively.

3   Ibid., 60.

4   E. W. Trueman Dicken, *The Crucible of Love: A Study of the Mysticism of St. Teresa of Jesus and St. John of the Cross* (New York: Sheed and Ward, 1963), 189.

5   Catherine Swietlicki, *Spanish Christian Cabala: The Works of Luis de León, Santa Teresa de Jesús, and San Juan de la Cruz* (Columbia, Mo.: University of Missouri Press, 1986), 68–69.

6   Ángel Raimundo Fernández, "Génesis y estructura de *Las Moradas del Castillo Interior*," in *Actas del Congreso Internacional Teresiano, Salamanca, 4-7 Octubre 1982,* eds. Teófanes Egido et al., 2 vols. (Salamanca: Universidad de Salamanca, 1983) 2: 609–36.

7   Víctor García de la Concha, *El arte literario de Santa Teresa* (Barcelona: Editorial Ariel, 1978), 264–74.

8   Juan Fernández Jiménez, "Sobre la estructura de las *Moradas del castillo interior*," in *La Chispa '81: Selected Proceedings of the Second Louisiana Conference on Hispanic Languages and Literatures, Tulane University, New Orleans, 1981,* ed. Gilbert Paolini (New Orleans: Tulane University, 1981), 107–15.

9   E. Michael Gerli, "El *Castillo interior* y el 'arte de la memoria,'" *Bulletin Hispanique* 86 (1984): 154–63; also published in *Santa Teresa y la literatura mística hispánica: Actas del I Congreso Internacional sobre Santa Teresa y la mística hispánica,* ed. Manuel Criado de Val (Madrid: EDI-6, 1984), 331–37. The basis of the art of memory is the imaginative organization of space and spatially arranged imagery. Its method consists in visualizing some kind of structure in space made of recognizable parts standing in fixed relations to one another and then associating or "placing" what one wishes to remember with the various parts of the structure. See Frances Yates, *The Art of Memory* (Chicago: University of Chicago Press, 1966).

10 Alison Weber, *Teresa of Ávila and the Rhetoric of Femininity* (Princeton, N.J.: Princeton University Press, 1990), 98–122.

11 The standard work on the imagery of light and darkness in Teresa's works is María Jesús Fernández Leborans, *Luz y oscuridad en la mística española* (Madrid: CUPSA Editorial, 1978), 53–152.

12 Cf. 3.2.4, 9, 12; 4.1.7; 4.3.2, 9; 5.4.1, 6; 6.5.1, 7; 7.1.5; 7.3.8; and 1.1.5; 2.1.11; 4.3.2, 3; 7.1.5, 7. The soul's inward movement is not a

descent in Frye's sense, because it does not involve a loss of identity and leads, paradoxically, to the luminous higher world of heaven rather than to the demonic night world. Cf. Alison Goddard Elliot, *Roads to Paradise: Reading the Lives of the Early Saints* (Hanover, N.H.: University Press of New England, 1987), 103–67. Catherine Swietlicki has recently noted that Teresa creates in the castle/soul a space that is "simultaneously open and immense yet also interior and private" rather than "a precisely delineated place" ("The Problematic Iconography of Teresa of Ávila's *Interior Castle*," *Studia Mystica* 11 [1988]: 37–47, especially 38). The idea of the soul's simultaneous upward and inward movement in mystical experience is not a new one in the Christian tradition. For example, it is found in St. Augustine, Hugh of St. Victor, and others. See Andrew Louth, *Origins of the Christian Mystical Tradition: From Plato to Denys* (Oxford: Clarendon Press, 1981), 138–39; and Jürgen Moltmann, "Teresa of Ávila and Martin Luther: The Turn to the Mysticism of the Cross," *Studies in Religion* 13 (1984): 265–78, especially 270.

13   See Ramón Menéndez Pidal, "El estilo de Santa Teresa," which, though originally published in *Escorial* in 1941, is most accessible in his *La lengua de Cristóbal Colón*, Colección Austral 280 (Buenos Aires: Espasa-Calpe, 1942), 129–53; Marcelle Auclair, *St. Teresa of Ávila*, trans. Kathleen Pond (London: Burns Oates, 1953), 324–25; María Rosa Lida de Malkiel, "La visión de trasmundo en las literaturas hispánicas," in Howard R. Patch, *El otro mundo en la literatura medieval*, trans. J. Hernández Campos (Mexico City: Fondo de Cultura Económica, 1956), 425–26; Cristóbal Cuevas García, "El significante alegórico en el *Castillo* teresiano," *Letras de Deusto* 12 (1982): 77–97, especially 91–97; and Francisco Márquez Villanueva, "El símil del castillo interior: Sentido y génesis," in *Actas del Congreso Internacional Teresiano* 2: 495–522, especially 499–500. Many other sources have been suggested for the image of the interior castle. For an overview of the formidable body of scholarship on this question as well as two further contributions to it, see Márquez Villanueva's article just cited and Luce López-Baralt, "El símbolo de los siete castillos concéntricos del alma en Santa Teresa y en el Islam," in her *Huellas del Islam en la literatura española de Juan Ruiz a Juan Goytisolo* (Madrid: Hiperión, 1985), 73–97.

14   See *Anatomy of Criticism,* 149 and Herbert Friedmann, *A Bestiary for St. Jerome: Animal Symbolism in European Religious Art* (Washington, D.C.: Smithsonian Institution Press, 1980), 293–96.

15   See Gen. 1.26–30; Boniface Ramsey, *Beginning to Read the Fathers* (New York: Paulist Press, 1985), 70, 152; and Elliot, 144–67.

16   See *Great Code*, 144–45 and Colleen McDannell and Bernhard Lang, *Heaven: A History* (New Haven, Conn.: Yale University Press, 1988), 119–22, 142–44.

17   John Welch, *Spiritual Pilgrims: Carl Jung and Teresa of Ávila* (New York: Paulist Press, 1982), 142–43.

18   Ibid., 142.

19   See Fernández Jiménez, 114, note 7; cf. Hatzfeld, 60.

20   In his *Introduction to the Devout Life*, pt. 3, chap. 2, St. Francis de Sales makes a similar point about supernatural favors, which, he says, are "slight indications of the happiness of the life to come. Sometimes they are granted to men to make them desire what is complete in heaven above" (trans. John K. Ryan [Garden City, N.Y.: Image Books, 1972], 126–27).

21   The temple is an archetype of the higher worlds. See *Great Code*, 156–60, 166.

22   The martial aspect of the fourth through seventh mansions has tended to be overlooked by scholars. See Elizabeth T. Howe, *Mystical Imagery: Santa Teresa de Jesús and San Juan de la Cruz* (New York: Peter Lang, 1988), 124.

Chapter 4 The *Foundations*

1   E. Allison Peers, *Mother of Carmel: A Portrait of St. Teresa of Jesus* (1944; Wilton, Conn.: Morehouse-Barlow, 1979), 140.

2   Ibid., 139.

3   Teófanes Egido, "*Libro de las fundaciones*" in *Introducción a la lectura de Santa Teresa*, ed. Alberto Barrientos (Madrid: Editorial de Espiritualidad, 1978), 241–68, especially 248–49.

4   Guido Mancini, *Teresa de Ávila: La libertà del sublime* (Pisa: Giardini Editori, 1981), 246–47.

5   Víctor García de la Concha, "Estudio introductorio" to his edition of Teresa de Jesús, *Libro de las fundaciones* (Madrid: Espasa-Calpe, 1982), 20–21.

6   Alison Weber, *Teresa of Ávila and the Rhetoric of Femininity* (Princeton, N.J.: Princeton University Press, 1990), 123–57.

7 Testimony no. 6 in *Collected Works of St. Teresa of Ávila*, I: 323.

8 Bede Edwards, "The Memoirs of a Gadabout," *Mount Carmel* 19 (1970): 61–76, especially 61.

9 García de la Concha, 20.

10 Ibid.

11 Peers, 65.

12 See Jean Leclercq, *The Life of Perfection: Points of View on the Essence of the Religious State*, trans. Leonard J. Doyle (Collegeville, Minn.: Liturgical Press, 1961), 119–25.

13 García de la Concha observes on p. 19 of his introductory study to *Libro de las fundaciones* (see note 5) that Teresa's emphasis on favors (*mercedes*) in the *Foundations* links it to the *Life*, which Teresa gave the alternative title "Of the Mercies (*misericordias*) of God" (*The Letters of St. Teresa of Jesus*, trans. E. Allison Peers, 2 vols. [1951; London: Sheed and Ward, 1980] 2: 889).

14 See Leclercq, 122 and Boniface Ramsey, *Beginning to Read the Fathers* (New York: Paulist Press, 1985), 153.

15 Kieran Kavanaugh identifies this nun as Petronila de San Andrés (Robles y Castro, 1545–1576), who was born in Toledo and professed there in 1571. See *Collected Works of St. Teresa of Ávila*, III: 424 (chap. 16, note 4).

16 In *The Complete Works of St. Teresa of Jesus*, trans. E. Allison Peers, 3 vols. (1946; London: Sheed and Ward, 1978) 3: 368–78, especially 371.

17 See Paul Meyvaert, "The Medieval Monastic Garden," in *Medieval Gardens*, ed. Elisabeth B. MacDougall (Washington, D.C.: Dumbarton Oaks, 1986), 25–53.

18 Kieran Kavanaugh, "Introduction" to the *Foundations* in *Collected Works of St. Teresa of Ávila*, III: 27. See also *Foundations* 10.3 and *Letters of St. Teresa of Jesus* 2:736, 806.

19 Cf. Weber's discussion of the interpolated stories of Catalina Sandoval y Godínez, Casilda de Padilla, and Beatriz de la Madre de Dios, 248–56.

20 See John E. Steinmueller and Kathyrn Sullivan, *Catholic Biblical Encyclopedia: Old Testament* (New York: J. F. Wagner, 1956), 210; K. A. Kitchen, "Carmel," in *The New Bible Dictionary*, ed. J. D. Douglas (1962; Grand Rapids, Mich.: Eerdmans, 1963), 200–201; G. W. Van Beek, "Carmel, Mount," in *The Interpreter's Dictionary of the Bible*, 4 vols. (New York: Abingdon Press, 1962) 1: 538; Louis Hartmann and L. Stolwijk, "Carmel," in the *Encyclopedic Dictionary of the Bible*, ed. Louis Hartmann (New York: McGraw-Hill, 1963), 324–25; and *The New Westminster Dictionary of the Bible*, ed. Henry S. Gehman (Philadelphia: Westminster Press, 1970), 150–51.

21 On the historical development of the Carmelites, see Joachim Smet, *The Carmelites: A History of the Brothers of Our Lady of Mt. Carmel*, 4 vols. (Darien, Ill: Carmelite Spiritual Center, 1975–85) 1: 1–23, 85–87; Bede Edwards' introduction to his edition and translation of *The Rule of St. Albert* (Aylesford: Carmelite Priory, 1973), 11–41; and David Knowles, *The Religious Orders in England*, 3 vols. (1948–59; Cambridge: Cambridge University Press, 1979) 1: 195–99.

22 In *Complete Works of St. Teresa of Jesus* 3: 371.

23 Jürgen Moltmann, "Teresa of Ávila and Martin Luther: The Turn to the Mysticism of the Cross," *Studies in Religion* 13 (1984): 265–78, especially 276.

24 Kavanaugh, "Introduction" to the *Foundations* in *Collected Works of St. Teresa of Ávila*, III: 12.

25 Carole Straw, *Gregory the Great: Perfection in Imperfection* (Berkeley, Calif.: University of California Press, 1988), 115.

Conclusion

1 James A. Wiseman, "Teaching Spiritual Theology: Methodological Reflections," *Spirituality Today* 41 (1989): 143–59, especially 147.

2 Frederick Hartt, *Love in Baroque Art* (Locust Valley, N.Y.: J. J. Augustin Publisher, 1964), 5.

3 Ibid., 6.

4 Ibid., 6–7.

5 Ibid., 8.

6 It is disappointing that Teresa's splendid imagery and theology of heaven are completely overlooked in Colleen McDannell and Bernhard Lang, *Heaven: A History* (New Haven, Conn.: Yale University Press, 1988).

7 Recently Jürgen Moltmann has observed that "[the] story of Teresa's life is the story of her soul with God, the story of the long search, of the discovery at last, and of the peaceful, confident life in God's fellowship. Looked at from the other side, it is the story of God with a soul, a story of courtship, of a call, of a 'bringing-to-oneself,' and of a final indwelling and repose of God in the soul" ("Teresa of Ávila and Martin Luther: The Turn to the Mysticism of the Cross," *Studies in Religion* 13 [1984]: 265–78, especially 269).

Annotated Bibliography

The purpose of this section is to provide neither an exhaustive Teresian bibliography nor a list of the works cited in this study. Rather it is make available a guide to selected—and recent—Teresian publications. With few exceptions, priority is given to items published since 1982, the fourth centenary of St. Teresa's death, since they are not included in existent Teresian bibliographies.

Texts

The Spanish text of Teresa's complete works is available in a handy one-volume edition prepared by Efrén de la Madre de Dios and Otger Steggink (7th ed., Madrid: Editorial Católica, 1982). This volume has a good bibliography of editions of Teresa's works as well as publications on Teresa's life and writings up to 1982. There are also some very fine recent editions of individual works, e.g., Dámaso Chicharro's edition of the *Life* (Madrid: Ediciones Cátedra, 1979) and Víctor García de la Concha's edition of the *Foundations* (Madrid: Espasa-Calpe, 1982). Both editions have good critical introductions. Additionally, Chicharro's has excellent bibliography and notes.

The classic English translation of Teresa's works is E. Allison Peers's *The Complete Works of St. Teresa of Jesus*, 3 vols. (1946; London: Sheed and Ward, 1978) and *The Letters of St. Teresa of Jesus*, 2 vols. (1951; London: Sheed and Ward, 1980). A more recent, and readable, translation is that of Kieran Kavanaugh and Otilio Rodríguez, *The Collected Works of St. Teresa of Ávila, I: The Book of Her Life, Spiritual Testimonies, Soliloquies; II: The Way of Perfection, Meditations on the Song of Songs, The Interior Castle*; and *III: The Book of Her Foundations, Minor Works* (Washington, D.C.: Institute of

Carmelite Studies Publications, 1976–85). These volumes contain reliable, informative, and very helpful critical introductions by Kavanaugh to each of the works translated.

Conference Proceedings and Special Journal Issues

The celebration in 1982 of the quatercentenary of Teresa's death resulted in a huge volume of scholarly publications. Symposia on Teresa were held on both sides of the Atlantic, and, subsequently, the proceedings of these conferences were published. Moreover, many journals dedicated one or more issues to Teresa. These proceedings and special issues contain papers that treat various aspects of Teresa's life and writings—historical, theological, spiritual, literary, psychological, and iconographic. The following is a list of some of the most significant collections of conference proceedings and special journal issues.

Boletín del Museo e Instituto "Camón Aznar" 10 (1982).

Criado de Val, Manuel, ed. *Santa Teresa y la literatura mística hispánica: Actas del I Congreso Internacional sobre Santa Teresa y la mística hispánica*. Madrid: EDI-6, 1984.

Egido, Teófanes, Víctor García de la Concha, and Olegario González de Cardedal, eds. *Actas del Congreso Internacional Teresiano, Salamanca, 4-7 Octubre 1982*. 2 vols. Salamanca: Universidad de Salamanca, 1983.

Letras de Deusto. Número extraordinario: IV Centenario de Santa Teresa (1582–1982) vol. 12 (1982), no. 24.

Rees, Margaret, ed. *Teresa de Jesús and Her World: Papers of a Conference Held at Trinity and All Saints College, 24-25 October 1981*. Leeds, England: Trinity and All Saints' College, 1981.

Revista de Espiritualidad. Nos. 159–60 (1981): Santa Teresa en su ambiente histórico. No. 161 (1981): Hombre y mundo en Santa Teresa. Nos. 162–63 (1982): Teresa de Jesús: Mujer, cristiana, maestra. No. 165 (1982): Psicología y teología en el *Castillo interior.*

Sullivan, John, ed. *Carmelite Studies 3: Centenary of St. Teresa. Proceedings of the Catholic University Symposium*. Washington, D.C.: Institute of Carmelite Studies Publications, 1984.

Teresianum (formerly *Ephemerides Carmeliticae*). Special double issue for the fourth centenary of the death of St. Teresa of Ávila, 33 (1982) nos. 1–2.

Vermeylen, Alphonse, ed. *Thérèse d'Ávila: Actes du colloque pour le quatrième centenaire de sa mort organisé en collaboration avec la Faculté de Théologie, Louvain, 10 Mars 1982.* Louvain-La-Neuve, Belgium: Presses Universitaires de Louvain, 1982.

Word & Spirit: A Monastic Review 4. Dedicated to St. Teresa of Ávila (1582–1982). Still River, Mass.: St. Bede's Publications, 1983.

Studies

Included here are studies that do not appear in the proceedings, collections, or special journal issues cited above.

Aldrich, J. Ruth. "Teresa, A Self-Actualized Woman," *Carmelite Studies 2* (1982): 81–94. A study of Teresa in light of Abraham Maslow's description of the self-actualized person that concludes that the saint was psychologically very healthy.

Bache, Christopher M. "A Reappraisal of Teresa of Ávila's Supposed Hysteria," *Journal of Religion and Health* 24 (1985): 300–315. Argues that the severe seizures Teresa experienced reflect not degenerative psychopathology but progressive movement toward higher states of consciousness.

Barrientos, Alberto, ed. *Introducción a la lectura de Santa Teresa.* Madrid: Editorial de Espiritualidad, 1978. A helpful handbook that offers an overview of Teresa's historical context and spirituality as well as essays on each of the saint's works.

Barton, Marcela Biro. "St. Teresa of Ávila: Did She Have Epilepsy?," *Catholic Historical Review* 68 (1982): 581–98. Examines the possibility that Teresa had a form of epilepsy known as temporal-lobe seizures that, while part of the development of her mysticism, did not detract from her service to the Church and God.

Bilinkoff, Jodi. *The Ávila of St. Teresa: Religious Reform in a Sixteenth-Century City.* Ithaca, N.Y.: Cornell University Press, 1989. A historical analysis of Teresa's reform in its social and religious context.

Brennan, Margaret. "Teresa of Ávila: '. . . Undaunted Daughter of Desire,'" in *Spiritualities of the Heart: Approaches to Personal Wholeness in Christian Tradition.* Edited by Annice Callahan (New York: Paulist Press, 1990), 114–29. Reflects on Teresa's teaching on prayer and reform as a critique of societal and cultural structures that militated against full human and spiritual liberation and integration in sixteenth-century Spain.

Burrows, Ruth. *Interior Castle Explored: St. Teresa's Teaching on the Life of Deep Union with God*. London: Sheed and Ward, 1981. A commentary by a contemporary Carmelite on Teresa's masterwork.

Chorpenning, Joseph F. "Images of a Saint: Three Recent Books on Teresa of Ávila," *Studia Mystica* 13 (1990): 77–87. A review-article of recent books on Teresa by Bilinkoff, Dubay, and Weber.

———. "The Monastery, Paradise, and the Castle: Literary Images and Spiritual Development in St. Teresa of Ávila," *Bulletin of Hispanic Studies* 62 (1985): 245–57. Offers an exposition of Teresa's method of image association and transference in the *Life*, the *Way of Perfection*, and the *Interior Castle* and suggests its significance.

———. "The Pleasance, Paradise, and Heaven: Renaissance Cosmology and Imagery in the *Castillo interior*," *Forum for Modern Language Studies* 27 (1991): 138–47. A development of some ideas presented in chap. 3.

Clissold, Stephen. *St. Teresa of Ávila*. London: Sheldon Press, 1979. A biography of the saint.

Culligan, Kevin. "Teresa of Jesus: A Personality Profile," *Spiritual Life* 29 (1983): 131–62. A study of Teresa's personality as revealed in her letters.

Davis, Elizabeth B. "De nuevo, sobre la 'literariedad' de Teresa de Jesús," *Anuario de Letras* (Mexico) 28 (1990): 159–80. Discusses the paradisal imagery of the *Life*, chaps. 11–22, and the various audiences Teresa addresses in the *Castle*.

Dombrowski, Daniel A. "Was St. Teresa a Shrew?" *The Downside Review: A Quarterly of Catholic Thought* 109 (1991): 35–43. A presentation of and response to William James's critique of Teresa in *The Varieties of Religious Experience*.

Dorgan, Margaret. "St. Teresa of Ávila: Woman and Waverer," *Cross Currents* 32 (1982): 155–59. A thoughtful essay on Teresa's first eighteen years as a nun and her conversion experience.

Dubay, Thomas. *Fire Within: St. Teresa of Ávila, St. John of the Cross and the Gospel—on Prayer*. San Francisco: Ignatius Press, 1989. A study of the major elements of the two Carmelite doctors' spiritual doctrine in relation to the teaching of Sacred Scripture.

Egan, Harvey D. *Christian Mysticism: The Future of a Tradition*. New York: Pueblo Publishing, 1984. On Teresa, see 118–64.

Egido, Teófanes. *El linaje judeoconverso de Santa Teresa: Pleito de hidalguía de los Cepeda.* Madrid: Editorial de Espiritualidad, 1986. Documents Teresa's Jewish descent.

García de la Concha, Víctor. *El arte literario de Santa Teresa.* Barcelona: Editorial Ariel, 1978. The most important book on Teresa's writings published during the past decade.

González-Casanovas, Roberto J. "Writing in St. Teresa as a Dialogue of Faith and Love: 'Mental Prayer' in *Camino de perfección* (chap. 24)," *Studia Mystica* 13 (1990): 60–76. Examines the importance of writing for Teresa as a self-conscious exercise in contemplation and as a virtuous action for the guidance of others.

Green, Deirdre. *Gold in the Crucible: Teresa of Ávila and the Western Mystical Tradition.* Shaftesbury, England: Element Books, 1989. Studies the influence of Jewish mysticism and the Christian Cabala on Teresa as well as examines her place in the Western mystical tradition and her importance for women's spirituality.

Herrero, Javier. "The Knight and the Mystical Castle," *Studies in Formative Spirituality* 4 (1983): 393–407. Discusses the formative influence of the romances of chivalry on the metaphors Teresa employs to express her religious experience.

Hollis, Karen. "Teresa de Jesús and the Relations of Writing," in *Conflicts of Discourse: Spanish Literature in the Golden Age.* Edited by P. W. Evans (New York: Manchester University Press, 1990), 26–47. Considers Teresa's gradual emergence and development as a writer as a function of a series of relationships between the writer, her texts, and the contexts in which she wrote.

Howe, Elizabeth Teresa. *Mystical Imagery: Santa Teresa de Jesús and San Juan de la Cruz.* New York: Peter Lang, 1988. A useful guide to the imagery of the two mystics, grouped according to six categories: fauna, flora, familiar objects, the body (social and physical), familiar activities, and the four elements.

Kavanaugh, Kieran. "St. Teresa and the Spirituality of Sixteenth-Century Spain," in *The Roots of the Modern Christian Tradition.* Edited by E. Rozanne Elder (Kalamazoo, Mich.: Cistercian Publications, 1984), 91–104. An essay on Teresa that situates her within the context of the spiritual trends of the Spain of her day.

Lapesa, Rafael. "Estilo y lenguaje de Santa Teresa en las *Exclamaciones del alma a su Dios*," in *Aureum Saeculum Hispanum: Beiträge zu Texten des Siglo de Oro.* Edited by Karl Hermann Körner and Dietrich

Briesemeister (Weisbaden, Germany: Steiner, 1983), 125–40. A study of Teresa's style and level of literary culture.

Lavin, Irving. *Bernini and the Unity of the Visual Arts*. 2 vols. New York: Pierpont Morgan Library and Oxford University Press, 1980. The best available study of Bernini's *Ecstasy of St. Teresa in situ* that contains much valuable information as well as an excellent bibliography on Teresian iconography.

López Baralt, Luce. "El símbolo de los siete castillos concéntricos del alma en Santa Teresa y en el Islam," in her *Huellas del Islam en la literatura española de Juan Ruiz a Juan Goytisolo* (Madrid: Hiperión, 1985), 73–97.

———. "Simbología mística musulmana en San Juan de la Cruz y en Santa Teresa de Jesús," *Nueva Revista de Filología Hispánica* 30 (1981): 21–91. This study and the previous essay point out coincidences between the imagery of Teresa and John and that of the Islamic mystics.

Lussier, Bonaventure. "Jungian Individuation and Contemplation in Teresa of Jesus," *Carmelite Studies* 4 (1987): 218–74. Traces Teresa's maturation process and journey to wholeness in the *Life*.

Mancini, Guido. *Teresa de Ávila: La libertà del sublime*. Pisa: Giardini Editori, 1981. A general introduction to Teresa's works.

Márquez Villanueva, Francisco. "La vocación literaria de Santa Teresa," *Nueva Revista de Filología Hispánica* 32 (1983): 355–79. A seminal essay on Teresa's desire to write and to be read.

Moltmann, Jürgen. "Teresa of Ávila and Martin Luther: The Turn to the Mysticism of the Cross," *Studies in Religion* 13 (1984): 265–78. A sympathetic appreciation of Teresa by a leading Lutheran theologian that identifies similarities and differences between Protestant faith and Carmelite spirituality.

Morón Arroyo, Ciriaco. "Sanctity/Sanity: A Study of St. Teresa's *Interior Castle*," *Studies in Formative Spirituality* 4 (1983): 187–99. A masterful study of the interrelationship of holiness and human wholeness in the *Castle*.

Morris, C. Brian. "The Poetry of Santa Teresa," *Hispania* 69 (1986): 244–50. Discusses an often neglected genre of Teresa's literary corpus.

Orozco Díaz, Emilio. *Expresión, comunicación y estilo en la obra de Santa Teresa: Notas sueltas de lector*. Granada, Spain: Diputación Provincial, 1987. A collection of essays on various aspects of Teresa's works.

Poitrey, Jeannine. *Vocabulario de Santa Teresa*. Madrid: Fundación Universitaria Española, 1983. A concordance of the *Life* and the *Way of Perfection*.

Rhodes, Elizabeth. "Reconsidering St. Teresa and Golden-Age Religious History," *Journal of Hispanic Philology* 14 (1990): 277–85. An important review-article of Weber's book *Teresa of Ávila and the Rhetoric of Femininity*.

Rhodes, Jan. "St. Teresa and Devotion to Christ's Passion: 'I am only asking you to look at Him,'" *Mount Carmel* 27 (1979): 108–37. An excellent study of Teresa's devotion to the Passion in the context of the religious culture of her day.

Ros García, Salvador. "Los estudios teresianos: Panorama de actualidad y perspectivas de tratamiento," *Teresianum* 38 (1987): 149–209. A survey of the state of Teresian scholarship.

Rossi, Rosa. *Teresa de Ávila: Biografía de una escritora*. Trans. M. Gargataglia and A. Domingo. Barcelona: Icaria Editorial, 1983.

Sánchez, Manuel Diego. "Bibliografía del centenario teresiano," *Teresianum* 34 (1983): 355–451. A useful, though incomplete, bibliography of publications that appeared in conjunction with the observance of the fourth centenary of Teresa's death.

Shank, Lillian Thomas, and John A. Nichols, eds. *Peace Weavers: Medieval Religious Women II*. Kalamazoo, Mich.: Cistercian Publications, 1987. Contains essays on Teresa's Christocentric spirituality, mystical prayer, and role as a spiritual guide and teacher.

Slade, Carole. "St. Teresa's *Meditaciones sobre los Cantares*: The Hermeneutics of Humility and Enjoyment," *Religion & Literature* 18 (1986): 27–44. Maintains that Teresa uses a hermeneutics defined as distinctively feminine to interpret the Song of Songs, thus making an argument for her right to teach the Word of God.

Smith, Paul Julian. "Writing Women in the Golden Age," in his *The Body Hispanic: Gender and Sexuality in Spanish and Spanish American Literature* (Oxford: Clarendon Press, 1989), 11–43. Studies Teresa's style from the perspective of the feminist criticism of Julia Kristeva and Luce Irigaray.

Sullivan, Mary C. "From Narrative to Proclamation: A Rhetorical Analysis of the Autobiography of Teresa of Ávila," *Thought* 58 (1983): 453–71.

Swietlicki, Catherine. *Spanish Christian Cabala: The Works of Luis de León, Santa Teresa de Jesús, and San Juan de la Cruz*. Columbia, Mo.: University of Missouri Press, 1986. Argues for Cabalist influence on Teresa's images of the castle, the silkworm, the nut, and the tree of life.

————. "The Problematic Iconography of Teresa of Ávila's *Interior Castle*," *Studia Mystica* 11 (1988): 37–47. A comparative analysis of Teresa's text and Fray Juan de Rojas y Ausa's 1677 book of emblems inspired by the *Interior Castle* that neglects the lengthy prose commentary that accompanies the emblems.

————. "Writing 'Femystic' Space: In the Margins of St. Teresa's *Castillo interior*," *Journal of Hispanic Philology* 13 (1989): 273–93. A psycholinguistic study of the *Castle* in its sociocultural context that takes issue with the work of Paul Julian Smith (see "Writing Women in the Golden Age").

Weber, Alison. *Teresa of Ávila and the Rhetoric of Femininity*. Princeton, N.J.: Princeton University Press, 1990. A study of the rhetorical strategy of the *Life*, the *Way of Perfection*, the *Interior Castle*, and the *Foundations*.

Welch, John. *Spiritual Pilgrims: Carl Jung and Teresa of Ávila*. New York: Paulist Press, 1982. A study of the imagery of the *Interior Castle* from the perspective of Jungian depth psychology.

Wilson, Christopher C. "Beyond Strong Men and Frontiers: Conquests of the Spanish Mystics," in *Temples of Gold, Crowns of Silver: Reflections of Majesty in the Viceregal Americas*. Edited by Barbara von Barghahn (Washington, D.C.: George Washington University, 1991), 116–27. A fine essay on the influence of Teresa's writings on Spanish colonial art.

Index

A

Ahumada, Beatriz de (Teresa's mother), 3, 4, 52
Almsgiving, 3
Amadís de Gaula, 22, 62, 98
Anatomy of Criticism: Four Essays, 24, 26, 49, 81, 85, 107
Andrew, St., 130
Anthony, St., 55, 66
Athanasius, St., 55
Augustine, St., 7, 10, 13, 14, 59
Augustinians, 10, 127
Ávila of the Knights, 2

B

Barnabites, 12
Beas (St. Joseph of the Savior monastery), 130
Black English, 10
Book of Her Foundations, 1, 13, 14, 20, 26, 69
   ascent to heaven, 119–23
   dual character of, 117, 118
   heroic defense of the earthly paradise, 132–40
   obedience, 120, 121, 122, 123, 128, 138, 139
   rapture, 138
   relationship to *Life, Way,* and *Interior Castle,* 118, 119, 124, 140
   restoration of the earthly paradise of the monastery, 124–32
   structure of, 118
   unity in, 117, 119, 140
   visions, 120, 129, 139
Book of Her Life, 1, 10, 13–14, 16, 20, 26, 74, 90, 95
   allegories in, 47, 61–63, 142
   an idyllic world, 51–53, 71
   ascent heavenward, 63–65, 118
   ascent to the earthly paradise of St. Joseph's monastery, 67–70, 76, 77, 101, 125
   ascent to the earthly paradise of the soul, 61–63, 71, 96
   as U-shaped story, 50, 71
   calls, 58, 59, 60, 67, 71, 101
   coherence in, 47, 142
   completion of the heroic quest, 70–72
   conflicts in, 59